HIDING IN THE OPEN

✡

D0779647

Hiding in the Open

A Holocaust Memoir

Sabina S. Zimering, M.D.

NORTH STAR PRESS OF ST. CLOUD, INC.

ISBN: 0-87839-171-1

First Edition, September 2001
Third Edition, January 2004

Printed in the United States of America by
Versa Press, Inc., East Peoria, Illinois.

Published by
North Star Press of St. Cloud, Inc.
P.O. Box 451
St. Cloud, Minnesota 56302

Dedication

To my mother and father and all the others brutally silenced.

To our Catholic friends: Mrs. Justyna, my grade school teacher, and her daughters, Danka and Mala, for giving my sister and me a chance to survive the Holocaust.

Acknowledgments

Writing my story was not easy, and it would have been more difficult if not for the support I received along the way. Bella Brodzki, my cousin's daughter, professor of Comparative Literature at Sarah Lawrence College, helped and encouraged me to keep writing from the very beginning. Burt Baum, a writing colleague, provided valuable feedback from the first class at the Loft until I finished my story. Paulette Alden, author and my superb creative writing teacher, and the other students call my work a "book." Paulette and my classmate and friend Kathy Vessels dedicated a lot of their time and effort in search of a publisher.

Members of my long-lasting book group: Hadassah Bacaner—who years ago showed interest in my war experience—Geraldine Braden, Audrey Larkin, Diana Lassman, Marjean Postlethwaite, Barbara Serrin, Ruth Stein—a children's book editor—and Taiko Tenaka added helpful observations and comments.

My editors Kristin Gallagher and especially Marc Niesen, with his insight and strong emphasis on expressing my feelings, helped the book come alive.

And, of course, my gratitude goes to my loving family. My husband, Ruben, remained steadfast when I was in doubt, and my daughter Rose's enthusiasm gave the often-needed boost. My son, Mark, helped me move from handwriting to the computer, and my youngest, Bonnie, with her beautiful English and creative mind, became my constant advisor. Friends and authors, Rena Coen and Edith Mucke, who had faith in my book, recommended it to their publisher, North Star Press.

Finally, I'd like to thank the Dwyer women of North Star Press for choosing my book, using good sense and working intensely to bring it to the readers.

Foreword

I finally made it to the creative writing class at the Loft Literary Center in Minneapolis. I had been thinking about writing my story for many years. I couldn't get it out of my mind, but to my family's disappointment, I continued to procrastinate: practicing medicine kept me too busy, the class was either the wrong day of the week or the wrong time of day, and traffic was heavy. Meanwhile, time kept passing. When I retired and lost the excuses, I gathered my courage and signed up.

I was the first one in this high-ceiling room and watched the other students, all women, walk in one by one. Looking around with some trepidation, each took a seat at the large wooden table, and the class began. We introduced ourselves, and the teacher, a woman around fifty with curly, auburn hair, explained certain aspects of creative writing. Then she said: "In the next ten minutes, write about anything that comes to mind." I panicked. Write instantly and be done in ten minutes? Still, I gave it a try. I wrote about making it to my first class. "All right, the ten minutes are up," the woman said. "Who would like to read her work?" A brave young woman raised her hand and began to read aloud. After a few sentences her voice broke, and she was sobbing. The class grew silent.

The teacher got up and walked slowly around the table. "This happens frequently and is a normal phenomenon when we write about painful events in our lives." But her comforting words didn't help, and the young woman couldn't go on. I felt sorry for her—and yet at the same time relieved. The classmate's tears and the teacher's words were just what I needed.

The class ended with a home assignment: "When I think of a memory, I think of . . ." That's exactly what I hoped to write. I wondered if my memory would serve me. It should. Many images never left my mind and are still vivid. But some might be vague, distorted or completely missing. Especially names. I shall try my best.

Poland

- International boundary
-·-·- Province *(województwo)* boundary
- ★ National capital
- ⊙ Province *(województwo)* capital
- Railroad
- Expressway
- Road

A province has the same name as its capital except where noted.

0   50   100 Kilometers
0   50   100 Miles

Lambert Conformal Conic projection, SP 40N/56N

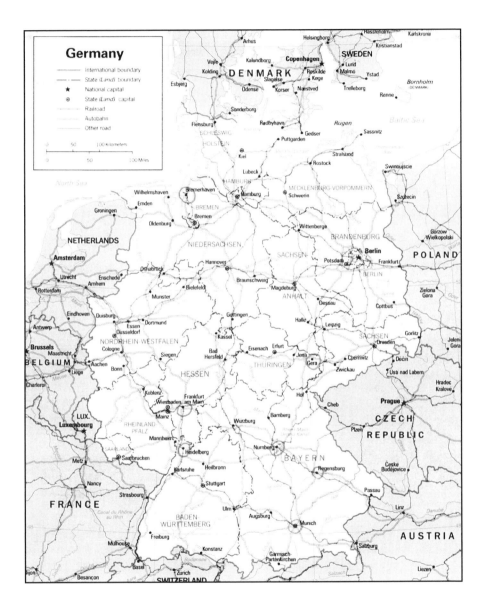

Germany

International boundary
State (Land) boundary
★ National capital
⊕ State (Land) capital
Railroad
Autobahn
Other road

0   50   100 Kilometers

0   50   100 Miles

DENMARK

Århus
Vejle
Kolding
Esbjerg
Kalundborg
Ødense
Slagelse
Korsør
Sønderborg
Flensburg
Kiel
Puttgarden
Rødbyhavn
Gedser

Helsingborg
Copenhagen
Roskilde
Køge
Næstved

SWEDEN
Hässleholm
Karlskrona
Kristianstad
Lund
Malmö
Ystad
Trelleborg
Rønne
Bornholm
(DENMARK)

Baltic Sea

Rügen
Sassnitz
Stralsund
Rostock
Swinoujscie
Szczecin

North Sea

Wilhelmshaven
Bremerhaven
Emden
Groningen
Oldenburg
Bremen

BREMEN

HAMBURG
Hamburg
Lübeck
Schwerin

MECKLENBURG-VORPOMMERN

NETHERLANDS
Amsterdam
Utrecht
Enschede
Arnhem
Rotterdam
Eindhoven
Duisburg
Essen
Düsseldorf

NIEDERSACHSEN
Hannover
Osnabrück
Bielefeld
Münster
Dortmund

Braunschweig
Magdeburg
Wittenberge

SACHSEN-ANHALT
Dessau
Halle
Leipzig

BRANDENBURG
Potsdam
Berlin
Frankfurt

BERLIN

Cottbus
Zielona Gora
POLAND
Gorzow Wielkopolski

Antwerp
Brussels
Maastricht
BELGIUM
Aachen
Liège
Charleroi

LUX.
Luxembourg
Metz
Nancy

Cologne
Bonn
Siegen
Göttingen
Kassel

Bad Hersfeld
Eisenach
Erfurt
Jena
Gera

NORDRHEIN-WESTFALEN

HESSEN

THURINGEN

Halle
Zwickau
Chemnitz
Dresden
Görlitz

SACHSEN

Jelenia Gora
Decin
Usti nad Labem
Hradec Kralove

Koblenz
Frankfurt am Main
Wiesbaden
Mainz

RHEINLAND-PFALZ

Hof
Cheb
Bamberg
Würzburg

Prague
Plzen
CZECH REPUBLIC

SAARLAND
Saarbrücken
Mannheim
Heidelberg

BAYERN
Nürnberg
Regensburg

Ceske Budejovice
Passau
Linz

Karlsruhe
Heilbronn
Stuttgart
Ulm
Augsburg
Munich

Strasbourg
Canal du Rhône au Rhin
FRANCE

BADEN-WÜRTTEMBERG
Freiburg
Konstanz
Bodensee
Garmisch-Partenkirchen
Salzburg
Liezen

AUSTRIA
Danube

Mulhouse
Basel
Zürich
SWITZERLAND

Dijon
Besançon

POLAND

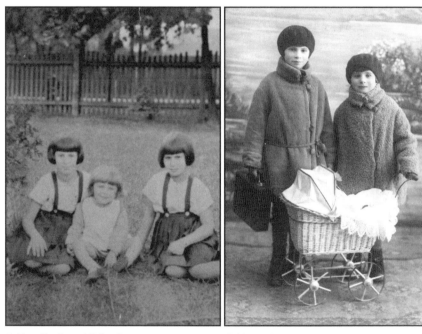

Sabina, Natek, and Helka. Pre-war.   Sabina and Helka.

1

September 1, 1939—a sunny Friday in my centuries-old hometown Piotrkow, Poland. In the crisp air, sounds had a special clarity, and golden leaves floated to the streets. Summer had quietly slid away, and fall had snuck in. I was glad. It had been the most boring of summers for me. Because of the widespread world Depression, money remained tight, and Father had decided, much to my disappointment, that we couldn't vacation in Przyglow. I had been waiting for it the whole year.

Przyglow was a village where Mother, my younger sister, Helka, little brother, Natek, and I spend the summers. Father took care of the coal business during the week and joined us on weekends. I loved everything there. The woods with the soft moss under my feet, the tall trees whispering to one another, and the lazy river where I swam and splashed with the teenagers from Lodz, a large city nearby. Once, I even joined their running race and won. A small bag of hard candy had been the award. I looked at it every day, proud of my accomplishment. One afternoon when a friend came to see it, I went to the cupboard and . . . the bag was open and half the candy gone. Mother had had unexpected guests.

The ballroom in the resort down the road was the most fun. Evenings, my girlfriends and I would go there to hear the loud music. With my face glued to the window, I couldn't take my eyes off the passionately dancing

Edzia, a high school classmate (perished in the war).
Przyglow, 1938.

young couples. But that summer I was stuck in Piotrkow, and my friends had all the fun. I wondered if any of them even missed me.

* * *

Friday, farmers' market day— since I had nothing better to do, I went along with Mother. Colorful flowers, fruits, vegetables, and restless chickens, ducks, and geese in wooden cages filled the wide-open space. I could hear the bargaining women from far away. While Mother, searching for the best buy, went from one farmer to the next, I wandered. The contrast between the delicate aroma of the flowers and the musty smell of horses palpably filled my nose. I reached out to pat the shiny coat of a pony when Mother pulled me away. "Sabka, let's go! It's almost noon. Father is waiting in the coal yard."

As we left the market, I helped with the heavy baskets and carried the live goose for the Shabbath dinner. With her feet tied, the frightened goose could only throw her graceful, long neck from side to side. Perhaps she knew what awaited her.

About half a block from home, a loud siren went off. Air raid. The alarms had been coming more and more frequently in the past few weeks. I had grown used to the warning to get off the street quickly, find a shelter and wait for the all-clear signal. How boring. I knew it by heart. As the wailing sound began to lose its strength, I detected a strange noise in the sky. I hardly had time to look up when I heard an explosive thunder. The ground shook underfoot. Bombs, real bombs. "Good," I whispered, "finally some excitement." I was sixteen, and boredom was my worst enemy.

Mother and I hid in the nearest building. A few minutes later, we dashed across the street to our own bomb shelter. Father, my sister, and brother already huddled in the basement. We squeezed in next to our neighbor, a widow with four unmarried daughters and a son. Ever since the son had been drafted into the Polish Army, she worried about his kosher food. An elderly couple in front of me held hands and exchanged loving whispers. A husky man, his face covered in sweat from digging ditches to defend our town, banged the door as he entered. He raised his fist to the sky and shouted: "Just wait, you damned Germans. We'll pay you back!" Many faces lit up. There was little love for Germans in our Polish town.

Overhead, I could hear the low flying planes circle again and again. With each pass, as the building shook with nearby explosions and glass shattered, I was sure they would hit us. If the three-story building collapsed, we wouldn't have a chance. At very least, I could be trapped in the rubble and suffocate. A slow suffocation. My fear grew. "Where is *Tata* [Father]?" I asked Mother. He crouched in the front of the basement and didn't hear me.

The sound of the bombers faded. We waited. Finally the all-clear siren, and I quickly ran up the stairs.

As the smoke and dust settled in the street, I could see that the entire wall had been blown off a nearby apartment building. A whimpering puppy raced back and forth on the window sill of an upper floor. He would come to the edge, look down and run back. The bombs had opened a gaping hole in the street. This added to the panic of the rushing men and women. A burning pile of coal near the power station threw a scarlet glow against the sky.

In the excitement and confusion, I heard that Romek, the eighteen-year-old neighbor I hoped would eventually notice me, had died in the bombing attack, struck by shrapnel as he stood on a balcony—our town's first victim.

And so the Second World War began.

2

The whole family quickly gathered at our grandparent's apartment on Krakowska Street, the old part of town.

Every Sunday we went there; these visits Helka and I loved and rarely missed. Most of the twelve grandchildren used to gather in Grandma's kitchen. We didn't dare disturb Grandfather, especially my sister and I, because it annoyed him that we spoke only Polish and not Yiddish. He brought this subject up to Father many times. Grandma didn't mind; she loved all of us.

Since television didn't exist in the thirties and radios were scarce, we made up our own entertainment at these gatherings. We told jokes, sang and danced. I was the dancer. I danced with feeling but in silence. No music accompanied me. My cousin Sara was the solo singer. She had a great voice and always knew the latest song. I would memorize it and, for the rest of the week, sing it over and over, till Mother complained, "Please stop it. I am getting a headache!"

I remember Grandma's kitchen had a squeaky wooden floor and a large coal stove. Sweets, fruits, and even a freshly baked cake awaited us. Sometimes she fixed my favorite dish—herring. She would wrap a whole herring in a newspaper and throw it on red, hot coals. Within minutes the herring was blackened, moist and crunchy. It was Grandma's specialty, and I never ate it anywhere else.

It saddened me that neither Grandma nor Grandpa ever ate in our house. They knew we weren't kosher.

* * *

When we headed to my grandparents' apartment that day after the sirens stopped, some aunts, uncles, and cousins had already arrived; others streamed into the house. Everyone looked anxious.

"What do we do? Wait out the attack? Head east?"

"We would have to reach the Soviet Union, far away. What should we do?" Everyone had questions.

Uncle Sam was the first to decide. His family would stay. "The Polish defense is strong, and the promised help of the French and English will stop the Germans. Why leave our home and go into the unknown?"

My father knew better and disagreed. He had followed Hitler's every move since he came to power. He knew about Hitler's military might and his hatred of the Jews. He hovered next to Grandpa's radio, tracking every detail of the news. I stood next to him. The daily programs had been replaced by war updates. Suddenly the room hushed. A reporter announced that France and England had just called an urgent meeting. They condemned Hitler's invasion of Poland, planned to honor their treaties and intervene. They declared war.

Moods rose.

"Will they push the Germans back?" I asked. "Will the war be over?"

Father looked skeptical. He continued to listen intently. The radio said the French and the English were only planning meetings. One meeting after another. No real word of intervention.

"We are leaving tonight," Father announced.

* * *

Squadrons of German warplanes, their tanks, and soldiers were conquering the country swiftly with no Polish forces in sight. Piotrkow, in the western part of the country, could fall any day. "We are leaving tonight," I whispered, repeating Father's words. I wondered where we would go and how we would get there. The few wealthy people with cars must have left already. Trains and buses were full; horse-drawn carriages hard to find. It had grown dark before Father found a grumpy driver with a horse that needed coaxing.

Grandma and Grandpa, two adult cousins, and our family of five squeezed into the carriage. Mother managed to add a couple of small suitcases with extra clothes and a few bundles with pillows and blankets, but it wasn't much.

"Hurry up, Sabka. We are ready to leave." Mother called. I ran to the basement with water and bread for the goose.

Pitch dark night. Yet, in the dark, the usually empty streets and country roads had filled with carriages, pushcarts, and people on foot. The pace was slow but urgent. Men, women, and children huddled close as they walked. An occasional cry for a lost child shook the air. We all headed east, towards the Soviet Union, but hundreds of kilometers lay between us and the border.

Adults in our crowded wagon tried to make plans. At first I listened, but the clip-clop of the horses' hooves and rocking of the carriage lulled me to sleep. A bump in the road startled me awake. Recent events raced through my mind. The colorful farmers' market, the falling bombs, the panic. And I had longed for excitement? Luckily only Mother had heard me wish for that at the start of the air raid.

*   *   *

Morning came before we reached Przyglow, my favorite summer place only ten kilometers away. The sun eased up over the pine trees, and the river shimmered. It brought back memories of visits of my best friends, Danka and Mala, daughters of my favorite grade-school teacher. In Przyglow, they had often been our guests.

Danka, who was my age, had brown eyes and a dark complexion. She was attractive, spunky, and

Danka (in back) and Mala. Pre-war Piotrkow.

strong-willed. Her sister, Mala, two years younger, had lighter skin and eyes and a gentler temperament. She would never dare contradict her sister whenever Danka would say, "*Jesus Christus,* Mala, don't you see you are wrong?"

My sister, Helka, and I were also just two years apart in age and resembled each other, with our brown eyes and hair. Somewhat shorter than I, Helka was pretty and far more determined than the petite, submissive Mala. I envied Danka her unquestioned authority over her sibling.

The four of us used to spend lots of time together. They came to our home, and we went to theirs. I liked theirs better. While we had a comfortable apartment, they had a two-story villa with an orchard and sprawling fields. In the summer, we picked sweet strawberries and, in the fall, crisp tart apples. We played hide-and-seek in the tall rye and wheat fields. We wove headbands and bracelets of delicate blue flowers.

I still remember Danka's bike. I didn't have one, and she had tried to teach me how to ride hers. On the quiet side street next to her home, I pumped the pedals, and she held the bike as she ran along. She must have thought I was able to ride on my own and let go of the bike. I crashed to the ground, scratched my knees and twisted the bike.

I also envied the new dresses and shoes she and Mala would receive for Christmas and Easter. When I complained about this, Mother would say: "Mr. and Mrs. Justyna are teachers and have a higher income than we do. Don't I buy you new dresses and shoes for Rosh Hashanah and Passover? They are just as nice even though less expensive."

* * *

When we pulled into Przyglow, it had become a refuge for the bewildered. Parents scrambled for food and shelter while tired children whimpered as they tagged along. After a short rest, we moved on. Grandma's ankle, which she had sprained getting out of the carriage, became swollen and painful. Father found another horse-drawn carriage, and our grandparents went back home. The cousins, two young men, wanting a faster pace, also left.

The five of us began a slow trek on foot. My brother, Natek, only eight years old, couldn't keep up, and Father carried him on his back a good part of the way. Our bundles felt heavier and heavier, and our pace slowed with each mile. Mother began to leave behind pieces of clothes, pillows, and blankets. The strewn possessions of others ahead of us cluttered the roads. I saw a stack of underwear, a toothbrush, and a doll in a beautiful dress but with tangled hair staring into the sky with her glass eyes.

* * *

Sulejow, a charming town five to six kilometers beyond Przyglow, was a nightmare. Without a sign of Polish Air Defense, the perfect formations of German bombers had the skies to themselves. They dropped firebombs and swooped low enough to machine gun people on the ground. As I lay motionless on the damp grass during one pass, I could see the face of the pilot inside a plane. Confusion and panic separated many families. Frantic mothers called for their children, and lost boys and girls searched in vain among rushing strangers. No one had time to help them. Smoldering houses gave off a choking stench. Dead horses lay split open next to the twisted, still-warm bodies of people. Black flies swarmed over them all. My little brother passed a dead boy with half-open eyes. "Mama, why is he lying here?"

"He got tired and is sleeping. Come on, Natek," Mother said, and she pulled him closer to her side.

* * *

In order to avoid the deadly planes, we began to walk at night and hide in the woods during the day. Occasionally, we passed tired soldiers marching slowly on foot. This was one of the few means of transportation the Polish Army had.

One quiet afternoon while our family rested in the woods, my sister and brother were stretched out on the soft moss sleeping soundly, while Mother and Father dozed against an old pine tree. I couldn't sleep. I looked at the four of them, and it struck me how young my sister and brother were and how old my parents were getting. Fear and exhaustion were visible on their faces even in their sleep. I felt I should be the one to look after all of them.

Suddenly a group of Polish soldiers came close. The officer gave a loud order. With no enthusiasm, the soldiers lifted their outdated rifles and began to shoot at the sky. I was sure the low-flying German planes would make a deadly response. I woke my family, and we swiftly moved away.

* * *

Changing days into nights and nights into days didn't help much. Walking in the dark on the bumpy dirt roads proved slow and tedious, especially for Father who carried Natek on his back for long stretches. In the daytime, German planes roared over our heads and made resting almost impossible. By the third day, I had had enough. Enough of trudging on wet, narrow paths with my shoes getting stuck in the mud. Enough watery soup, stale bread, and sleeping in barns. The next morning after yet another damp, windy night of walking, we found ourselves at the same place we had left the evening before. We had taken a wrong turn.

"Enough," I cried. "I want to go home to my bed and Mama's soup!"

"Me too, me too," whimpered Helka and Natek.

"We can't go home," said Mother. "Not yet. We will try to do less walking and find better farms."

At dusk when the planes stopped coming, Mother, who had Aryan looks, a dignified manner and spoke accent-free Polish, approached a respectable-looking farm. The owner and his family were quite friendly. In exchange for clothes from our bundles, they provided a good, hot meal—a thick beef stew, coarse farmer's bread, a platter full of mashed potatoes, and milk still warm from their cows. They spread straw mattresses on the kitchen floor and even allowed us to wash up in their large bowl. My sticky body needed it badly. The cold water and small piece of soap did wonders.

The next morning, we lingered. Our parents talked to the landowner and his wife while their children proudly showed us their animals. A horse licked the shiny coat of its wobbly foal, and a litter of kittens pounced on one another in a pile of straw. Suddenly the mare jerked her head, her eyes wide.

Loud voices in the distance. We quickly joined our parents. A neighbor ran toward us shouting, "They here! The Germans are here! They just came out of the forest."

A group of farmers gathered to hear the news. They were agitated and talked loudly. Father remained silent, his face ghostly white. He knew what to expect.

3

Hitler caught up with us in that small village.

When the rumbling grew louder and the ground shook, the landlord's family hurried inside, and we hid in the attic. Father, crouching below the small window, watched with horror. Curious, I wanted to see, and he let me peek through the smudged glass. Tanks, heavy artillery, and trucks full of soldiers in helmets with ready guns passed slowly by the farm. Fine dust lifted off the unpaved road.

"Take a quick look and move away," Father husked.

The soldiers focused their guns on every path between barn and the farmhouse. They even glared at the barking dogs.

"How dare they just march in!" I said.

"That's enough " said Father and pulled me back.

In the deserted village, only occasional shots broke the silence. For us, escape had ended. A whole week we had wandered night after night, from one strange village to another. Yet we had advanced only thirty kilometers, nowhere near the Russian borders. No longer able to stay ahead of the Germans, Father's hope vanished. There was nothing left for us to do but turn around. The roads again filled, this time with disheartened families heading home.

Piotrkow looked only slightly more damaged than when we had left, and our apartment had remained intact. The goose in the basement still lived.

Yet, it felt strange. Piotrkow, my familiar hometown, had changed. The scarlet patch against the sky from the burning coal pile disturbed the darkness of the nights. It remained there for many weeks, looking ominous.

One night, Mother woke me. "You're talking in your sleep again."

I blinked at her. "What did I say?"

"I heard only: 'Why?' and 'What next?'" I knew the rest. Why were the Germans so cruel to us and what's next to come?

The slow pace of the town had given way to frenzy. No one stopped to chat anymore. People hurried, always wide-eyed. German soldiers stood everywhere. I could hear their heavy boots on the cobblestones, the laughter and shouting in their strange language. They crowded all the stores repeating: *"Alles ist spott billig!"* ["Everything is dirt cheap!"] They bought or took anything they wanted. Liquor stores were most popular. The Germans were jubilant; all of us mourned.

Poland was not a free country anymore. It was occupied, the east by the Russians, the west by the Germans. And it all had happened in no more than two weeks. Only Warsaw held out a little longer. Hitler's *Blitzkrieg*—the lightening war—was over.

* * *

Piotrkow, circa 1930. Father, Helka, Mother, and me.

At first the Germans treated the Jews and the Poles the same, but soon large placards began to appear on kiosks, wooden fences, the walls of buildings, even on lampposts. *"Achtung, Achtung, alle Juden!* [Attention, attention, all Jews!] *Herr* [Mr.] *Kommandant* [orders under penalty of death] . . ." and a long list of demands followed. The demands came one at time, and the minute a new placard appeared a crowd formed instantly. Father was always there and brought home the news. His face told me our situation grew worse with each notice. Confiscation of Jewish businesses, large sums of money, jewelry, and furs came first. White armbands with a blue Star of David had to be worn by everyone but small children. The closure of Jewish schools. Soon thereafter, curfews.

A few weeks after the German occupation began, my high school friend Guta and I walked at dusk in a busy downtown street. She talked about

her father, who escaped to Russia, and left them (her mother and a younger brother) behind. He assumed as everyone else did, that only Jewish men were in danger by the Germans. I described our family's week-long wanderings.

Suddenly a uniformed policeman loomed in front of us. "What are you doing here? Don't you know about the curfew for the Jews? Follow me."

Late that night, Mother, in obvious fear, paid the penalty. It was my first encounter with German law and jail.

Rumors about the ghetto began to circulate.

Guta Fisch (perished). Piotrkow, September 1939.

* * *

"Moving into the ghetto, to the old, run-down part of town? How dare they? I like it here," I said, complaining to Mother when I heard the news.

Our apartment was the only home I had ever known. On the second floor of a three-story building on Narutowicza Street, we shared the building with some twenty families, most of them with children. Close to the park,

Father's coal yard, and our grade school, the apartment building had been convenient and comfortable. The backyard, with little grass but plenty of hard dirt, was large and noisy. Kids, big and small, nice or tough, had played there, shouting and laughing. Most of the games we had played, we made up ourselves. We had no strict rules, no uniforms, no equipment. The backyard would quiet down in the evening only after the mothers called again and again to get us to bed.

Our apartment, considered above average, had a small entry hall, a kitchen, and two rooms. The kitchen had little free space because of the large coal stove, the table, cabinet for pots and pans, and a sink with no running water. The water, which Mother boiled before we drank, was stored in a large white container. A narrow bed for our maid had been squeezed in between the window and the cabinet. As Uncle Sam frequently joked, our maids were never young or pretty. "Tola plays it safe and hires only the old or unattractive women," he would say.

Helka and I greeted every new maid hired with great expectations. We eagerly wanted to know if she would tell a story, or sing a song about a young, naive country girl with a broken heart wronged by a no-good man. I loved the long winter evenings in the kitchen with Maria or Anna chatting as she plucked the goose feathers, which became our down pillows and comforters. I didn't mind the tiny, fluffy feathers settling on my clothes and in my hair. The red coals in the stove threw flickering lights on the walls and the ceiling and filled the kitchen with cozy warmth. Sitting on our low stools, Helka and I looked up to the maid and waited for the mesmerizing song or story. I could never understand why Mother didn't keep the maids we admired most.

The room next to the kitchen served as our living room, dining room, and my bedroom. The sofa against the wall became my bed at night. A glass-enclosed china cabinet held the fancy dishes Mother rarely used. The large, solid table in the middle of the room was the center for everything. We all ate there, my sister and I did our homework there, and our parents talked about the coal business.

Every winter, the old ceramic oven in the right corner of the room regained its importance. Built into the wall between the living room and the bedroom, it stretched all the way from the floor to the ceiling. It took some effort to get it going. The maid or, during the Depression, one of us, would pull out a bucket full of the gray powdery ashes, empty it outdoors and carry the coal and

15

wood from the basement to our apartment, two flights up. After lighting a match, it took some blowing before the wood caught fire and it was safe to shut the iron door. We waited, it seemed forever, for the shiny tiles to get warm. I loved to slide my cold hands up and down the front of the oven, put my cheek against it and rub my back on the smooth, warm surface. No matter how freezing cold it was outdoors, the old ceramic oven kept us warm for a good twenty-four hours.

The adjoining room was the family bedroom. It had what seemed to me then, a huge bed, a crib, and an armoire for our clothes. The large windows, with the clusters of deep-red geraniums Mother loved and maintained all year, faced the open space and gave the apartment a bright, pleasant feeling. I was happy there. When, a short time before the occupation, Mother said to Father, "We should look for a larger place. The girls are growing up, we need something more presentable," I secretly did not agree.

I do remember that Helka and I winked and giggled. We knew Mother meant that we would soon be dating and would want to invite young men to our apartment. Still Father objected to the idea of a move. "Not now," he told Mother. "We barely made it through the tough times."

*   *   *

And I wondered about Father's coal business, whether the Germans would take it away from him. It was our only source of income. For years he had been doing quite well, but when the Depression hit, he plummeted from being a successful wholesaler to a shaky retailer.

Our coal yard, located a block from home, occupied a narrow strip of land squeezed between two buildings. Black coal of various sizes was piled up against the walls. I liked the large chunks the best because they glistened in the sun. The pieces of wood, fire starters, Father stored in a small shed. A true family business, Mother was an active partner, and my sister and I filled in when needed. Our little brother played there. The coal yard made me feel important. Everybody needed coal. It was the only way to cook and keep warm in the winter. I felt like a grown up when I took care of the customers. I knew how to use the huge scale, add and subtract, and where to keep the money. But one evening I disappointed my father. Alone in the small office, by the dim light of the kerosene lamp, I was absorbed in Tolstoy's *Anna Karenina*. The outside yard was dark and quiet. Suddenly Father came back. "How much did that man who just left pay for his coal?" he asked.

"Which man, what coal?"

I had not seen nor heard anyone. Father did not say much, but I knew he thought it wouldn't have happened if Helka had been there.

Helka really loved to be in the coal yard, even if it meant not finishing her homework. One time she found Father's old notebook with accounts not paid for years and insisted on collecting the debts. Father could never say no to customers asking for credit. The same people knew how to avoid our Mother. Now they had to deal with Helka. When a customer would tell her, "My husband isn't home; come back next week," she would return again and again. Most everyone got tired of this little nuisance and paid. Father was proud of Helka.

We also had a pet in the coal yard, a reddish-brown, slightly lame chicken. I don't remember whether she had a name. She stayed with us a long time. When she saw any of us come in, she squatted on the ground, and clucked and cackled with excitement until we picked her up. I loved to hold her, slide my hand over the soft feathers and whisper in her ear.

Father's lunch, which he ate in the small office, was her favorite meal. When she saw him eat, she flew to the top of the table and moved close to the food. She didn't care for his cottage cheese, sour cream, or the cucumber. Her target was the bread. With her sharp beak striking fiercely, she tore apart a whole slice of bread in no time at all. She ate it just as quickly. With her stomach full, she cocked her head, glanced at Father with her tiny, clear eyes and jumped down. Father, generally not an animal lover, considered her very special. The coal yard was her territory; she barely tolerated the customers. One morning, she didn't greet him. All of us looked for her, but we never saw her again. I didn't want to know what might have happened to her.

*   *   *

While I complained about leaving our home, Mother had been quietly getting ready to move into the ghetto. She sold or gave away most of our possessions. The one thing I wish she had kept was her green shawl. I loved that shawl. So large and soft. Its slightly bulging, round pieces of delicate wool reminded me of seashells. The dark-green silk wove them into long straight lines. The same shiny threads became long fringes at the bottom of the shawl. When Mother walked, these swayed gracefully from side to side. She used to wear the shawl for special occasions. It made her look elegant.

I often sneaked into the bedroom, pulled the shawl out of her drawer and threw it over my left shoulder. I became a dancer. I danced a passionate tango, no partner needed. The softness of the delicate wool and the fading aroma of Mother's perfume made me feel seductive.

And now I didn't even know who had the shawl.

4

"ere, Sabka, pack your things," she said and handed me a small sack. "Put what you want to leave behind on the bed."

Leave behind? I didn't want to leave anything behind. I didn't even want to move.

"Start with your school papers. They take the longest."

Mother was right. I got lost in my grade-school notebooks. Classmates, teachers, and the handsome priest came to life.

Before the war in Poland, religion (mostly Catholic) was not separated from the state. During the six years of grade school, I attended in our neighborhood, a priest taught the Catechism. The young, tall man in a long black robe made an impact on all of us, especially on the older girls, the minute he entered the class twice or three times a week.

As a Jew, I could go home, play in the schoolyard by myself or remain in class. I had tried home and the school yard—boring. I remained in class. Non-Catholics were not expected to do homework or take exams. I just listened. Frequently, though, when the priest asked a question, my hand went up. I became quite familiar with the Catholic religion. One day, on his way home, the priest stopped at our coal yard and tried to encourage my parents to send me on to the gymnasium. At that time, only grade school was compulsory and free. To go further in school, I would have to go to the gymnasium, a private and expensive prep school.

19

Piotrkow, circa 1934. Grade School. Mrs. Justyna sits in the middle. Sabina stands directly behind her.

I must have been seven or eight when a couple classmates asked me to become Catholic. "We are having so much fun together," they said. "Why don't you come to our priest and become one of us?"

It made sense to me. I didn't know too many Jewish kids, and those I knew I didn't like. They looked different to me and had a funny accent. I went home and asked my mother. She looked at me . . . and laughed. I felt embarrassed. I never asked again.

Helka and I admired the Christmas trees of our Catholic friends and sang Christmas carols with neighborhood girls. On Passover we exchanged our *matzo* for their colorful Easter eggs and watched a priest in a long, white robe sprinkle holy water on the festive Easter food spread out on the tables. He had to bless all of it before Catholics could eat it.

* * *

We did move into the ghetto where, from then on, only Jews lived. Father had to give up the coal yard, and Mother gave up our home. They assigned our family of five to a single sublet room with a family who didn't want us. To get to our room, we had to pass their living room, their bedroom, and the bedroom of a ninety-year-old grandmother. Bedridden, she moaned constantly and called for her daughter. Her stench seeped into our room. We annoyed the apartment owners whenever we came in or left. I even heard them argue about us. I dreaded to walk by them.

One day, Father came up with an idea: "Since the apartment is on the main floor and our window wide enough, why don't we use it as a door?" From then on, we went in and out as many times as we wanted without troubling the family. Only Mother had to struggle.

At first I hated our small room, the apartment owners, and the crowded, narrow streets of the ghetto. The wide streets, the park, Father's coal yard, and the neighborhood kids with whom I grew up—only few blocks away—had become unattainable now. The Germans had cut me off from my world.

There was no way out, and slowly I got used to it. Father's parents and the five of us lived in the same building. Part of Grandfather's pre-war apartment was taken up by his workshop, leaving no space for us. Their kitchen became the family's gathering place. During the curfew hours, Grandpa, Grandma, single Aunt Sally, and my parents would spend long evenings together.

I got to know my grandma better and loved the times I spent alone with her. Even though she spoke only Yiddish and I spoke mostly Polish, we understood each other.

I remember one of her stories. One day, Grandma, still a young country girl, walked alone through the meadow next to the forest. Suddenly a wolf came out of the woods and headed in her direction, not too close but moving briskly. Grandma was petrified. There was no house nearby and running away would only catch the wolf's attention. Her panic grew. Luckily, she noticed a small hole in the ground, jumped in and covered herself with the large dark shawl. A few minutes later, she heard the wolf saunter by.

I remember Grandma as a slight and fragile-looking woman, her small build matched with fine features. As a wife of an *Hassid* (an orthodox, religious Jew), she shaved her head and wore a wig of nondescript color and rough texture. I never saw her natural hair. She spent most of her time in the kitchen, her favorite spot being a chair between the stove and the table. That's where she worked and ate. Only the Friday night and Saturday meals did she eat in the dining room with Grandpa, whom she adored.

I remember sharing my worries with her about the approaching graduation exams. A diploma from the gymnasium was essential for any further studies. Already then, I knew I wanted to study medicine. The human body and soul fascinated me. Biology, psychology, and literature were my favorite subjects.

Father considered my wish unrealistic. Medical schools were expensive, and the studies took many years. He called it a road too long and too costly for us. He felt that teaching should be my profession. "Mr. and Mrs. Justyna [Danka and Mala's parents], both teachers, have secure jobs and very good income. They have none of the worries I have in the coal business. You should think about it."

I did think about it, but I didn't like it. I wanted to study medicine.

"There's plenty of time. We don't have to decide now." Mother said.

The Jewish gymnasium I had finished in June 1939 fell short of some credentials, and our class had to take the written and oral exams in a Polish school with strange teachers. The exam material would arrive in sealed envelopes from the Ministry of Education in Warsaw. It was scary. Grandma assured me that everything would be fine. She said she would pray for me. Half of our class failed. I made it. I was sure her prayer did it.

My last memory of Grandma was during the war. I think it was the end of 1941 or beginning of 1942. We already had lived in the ghetto, in the same building as our grandparents. Ill, Grandma ran a temperature, and her cough had worsened. She became thin and weak. Her doctor considered pneumonia or tuberculosis. His house calls and medications did not help. She died quietly. A small funeral procession walked briskly on a gloomy day. The cold wind sneaked under my clothes and sent shivers through my body. Clumps of wet leaves stuck to my shoes and made me lag behind the rushing mourners. The whole world's tears came down as fine drizzle. When they lowered Grandma into the deep, freshly dug hole, I couldn't look at the heavy dirt falling on her. It was cruel to leave her there alone.

At the time, none of us would have believed that Grandma would be the last member of our large family to have a funeral and her own grave at the Jewish cemetery in Piotrkow.

* * *

Grandfather, a small, slender man, had a strong will and confidence. He kept his long white beard, *yarmulka* (skullcap), and long black garment impeccably neat and clean. He ran a successful tailor business. The buzzing sewing machines and the chatter of the young apprentices made his apartment exciting to me. I loved to watch him work. He would reach for a large piece of cloth and spread it on the table. As his hands moved the heavy scissors quickly and confidently, the cloth took on the shape of a jacket, slacks, or coat. It happened so fast. He was a master. But I still worried that the smoothly gliding scissors might take the wrong direction.

As an *Hassid*, Grandfather prayed daily and was devoted to his rabbi. His *Shtibel* (small synagogue) comprised a sparsely furnished, two-room apartment. The rabbi and men used the large front room; the smaller one remained for women and children. Mothers and children could only see the backs of the praying men. With the *yarmulkas* on their heads, long black garments and the *tal'lis* (tasseled prayer shawls) over the shoulders, the men rocked back and forth. Grandfather and the rabbi led the service. On *Yom Kippur* (the Day of Atonement), Grandfather's mournful *Kol Nidre* song and Mother's tears moved me. Most Jewish families belonged to a *Shtibel*; most spoke mainly Yiddish.

Piotrkow had a large, official synagogue. First built in 1689, it had been destroyed and restored many times. On the main floor—spacious with stained glass windows and a high ceiling—only men prayed. Women and children prayed in the balconies. Most of the synagogues in Poland were Orthodox. Rabbi Moshe Lau, the father of the present chief rabbi of Israel, was the leader. I attended some of the services with the students and professors of our Jewish gymnasium. I remember one or two Polish military officials sitting in prominent seats. That made everyone uneasy. Rabbi Lau had to deliver his sermon in Polish.

In 1939, after the Germans occupied Piotrkow, they forbade the Jews to assemble, even in small groups. All prayers were said at home. After destroying the holy objects, they turned the beautiful synagogue into a storage place for their war supplies.

* * *

Only occasionally I would join my parents and grandparents. Living in a building with other teenagers proved exciting. I loved the small courtyard and the curfew evenings, especially after a boy from Lodz had kissed me . . . my very first kiss. I stopped envying the girls who had boyfriends. I was almost seventeen and ready for romance. The books I had read and the movies I had seen prepared me for it. Before the war, my friend Guta and I took long walks on Slowacki Avenue, Piotrkow's main promenade. Each of us looked for a handsome boy and tried to catch his attention. We walked back and forth. If the boy I liked smiled, my expectations soared. If he ignored me, I wouldn't give up and continued to think about him. I was good at daydreaming. After I had been kissed, I didn't need to daydream. David was real. Mother smiled, and Helka teased me when I tried to put together the best outfit and fussed over my hair. And I wasn't cranky any more. I was in heaven.

As I began to accept the loss of the Polish part of town, the nearby church bells would bring back memories, vivid memories of the two sisters, Danka and Mala, and Helka and me. The four of us had spent many happy days in the park next to Saint Bernard Church with its deep, resonating bells, across the street from our coal yard.

I loved kicking the rustling fallen leaves and collecting the brown chestnuts. They had soft, shiny surfaces and came in different sizes and shapes. I took them home, pretended they were chunks of coal and created my own coal yard. Danka and I were the owners, Helka and Mala the customers. No credit allowed.

Spying on young couples was the most fun. After we tracked down a young man and woman on a remote park bench, we would tiptoe from behind, watch them hug and kiss and run off shouting: "They are kissing! They are kissing!" The man would jump up, raise his fist, but the young woman, trying to button her blouse, would pull him away. They were gone in no time.

I also loved summer visits to Przyglow. We would begin the day with the beach. We splashed and swam in the slow lazy river and admired the teenagers from the Lodz summer camp. On the way home, we searched for wild mushrooms and berries, which dotted the thick forest. The small, yellow mushrooms with their slender stems and flat, round tops looked like umbrellas and loved the shade, while the tiny red strawberries soaked up the sun. If we found enough of them, Mother would fix our favorite summer lunch: sautéed mushrooms with crusty, buttered bread and sweet, wild strawberries with fresh cream. At night it took us forever to fall asleep as we talked and giggled in the large bed the four of us shared.

In all the years of our friendship, it had made no difference to any of us that Danka and Mala were Catholics and Helka and I Jews. Until the Germans occupied Piotrkow. The separation was quick. My sister and I went into the ghetto, Danka and Mala into the Polish underground movement.

5

Since Jews were not allowed to assemble, even in small groups, Father's favorite Sunday get-together in the Town Square ended. He missed exchanging business and political news with his friends. Every one considered him an expert in politics and valued his opinion.

Shortly after the Germans occupied Poland, they closed Jewish schools. Though illegal, we found ways to continue our education. I gave private lessons to grade-school children in their homes using Mrs. Justyna's instruction books. Natek was one of my students, but he didn't take me seriously. Two young daughters of a baker became my favorite pupils. The girls showed an eagerness to learn, and their father paid with bread and rolls. With food rationing in effect and frequent scarcities, fresh loaves of bread and crisp rolls delighted all of us.

I also managed to continue my own education. Several friends and two teachers met illegally. Our teachers, a husband and wife in their forties, had been professors at Lodz or Warsaw (I am not sure which). She, petite and gentle, taught math, physics, and chemistry, and he, muscular with thinning hair, taught the liberal arts subjects. In their small, well-kept apartment, books lay everywhere: on the shelves, the furniture, and on the floor. Our classroom consisted of a small table. We had no blackboard, no maps, nor equipment for chemistry experiments. I don't remember where we got the worn textbooks we used when we met several times a week. We had to be very cautious. We made sure to arrive and leave one at a time. Before I entered or left the building, I looked around for Germans, policemen, or worse yet, the Gestapo. While one teacher ran a class, the other stood guard.

One day in the middle of a math class, I heard beautiful whistling outside. Was it the opera *Carmen?* Before I could tell, the lady teacher jumped up and ran to the window. She turned to us: "Please put all the books into the top drawer. Szymon and Henryk, grab the tools and work on the broken chair. You girls, come to the kitchen."

Ada was to peel potatoes, and I started washing the dirty dishes. We waited. We waited for the loud German swearing, the heavy boots, and pounding on the door. Tension bit into our minds. A turning key broke the silence.

Ada (perished)

The husband poked in his head. "I'm sorry. I saw two German soldiers head in our direction. I decided to warn you. But they passed our entrance and kept going." The professor wiped the sweat of his face. Ada and I took off the aprons, and our friends put away the tools. Lessons continued.

Another session remains still vivid in my mind. As usual, I was sitting next to Ada, the daughter of my Hebrew teacher from before the war, a girl I liked a lot. Of medium-build, she had dreamy, brown eyes and long well-cared-for braids. I was writing in my notebook when I glanced at her. A louse with a full, large belly and short legs was steadfastly moving across her forehead. I glanced again. It was true. The louse was there. I froze, not knowing what to do. If I told her, she could sweep off the louse before anyone noticed it. But I might embarrass her. I kept on writing. Shortly, everyone could see the louse. We all kept quiet.

Ada and I became close friends. A year younger than I, I found her to be a sweet, sensitive girl. We got together quite often and dreamed about falling in love. Most of the time we met in her apartment, their spacious, pre-war apartment. I didn't want her to see our cramped place. We always had things to talk about: a book we had read, a girl we knew, who found a boyfriend, or a couple breaking up. I clearly remember Ada once saying, "I have so much love inside of me. If I could only find someone to give it to."

Her wish did not come true. Ada perished in Treblinka.

* * *

I again broke the law when I joined what was meant to be a history and philosophy group. The *Hashomer Hazair*—a Zionist Youth Organization—held meetings, organized and conducted by Jacob, in a private home, which carried the same risk as the classes with our professors and required extreme caution. Several years older than I, Jacob, a tall, thin (undernourished) young man, proved to be a serious, idealistic, and inspiring leader. One day, after only a few meetings, he announced: "Enough of philosophy and history. Let's face reality. The Germans are achieving their goal of the total annihilation of the Jews. Shouldn't we be doing something about it?" and he unveiled the plan of forming a resistance movement. The appeal was scary but exciting. More details were supposed to come. They never did. Jacob was arrested and vanished.

Hanka (perished)

The other leader of the Piotrkow Zionist Youth Organization was Hanka (Hanna), my favorite cousin, the younger of Aunt Yadzia and Uncle Sam's two daughters. Because of hard times even before the war, only Sara, the older one, had attended the business school.

Hanka trained to be a seamstress. She hated the work. Her mind and

28

heart bent to books. She read all the time and even made lists of great books for me. She decided to study on her own: Latin, philosophy, history, and science. Determined and compassionate with a clear focus in life, she became my role model. In spite of her mother's pleas, Hanka had wanted to immigrate to Palestine. The outbreak of the war stopped her.

The two of us continued to meet in the crowded, dirty ghetto. We found a spot where a few spindly trees replaced the extensive pre-war parks and meadows we had known. They told us the time of year. Swelling buds bursting open meant spring, and, when the leaves grew wide enough to give us shade, we called it summer. The change of color let us know when fall arrived, with winter just around the corner. When fresh fluffy snow covered the branches and intricate snowflakes glittered in the sun, the trees took on a haunting beauty. Nature, ignoring the misery around it, went on with its seasons and cycles of life. This tiny oasis gave Hanka and me inspiration and hope.

6

I t had been more than a year since the Germans occupied Piotrkow and forced us into the ghetto. Then they made Krakowska Street off limits for the Jews. Our grandparents, David and his family, and we had to move. Scattered throughout the small ghetto, we rarely saw each other after that. Displaced families with bundles on their backs streamed in from the neighboring towns and villages. An old, run-down building with no teenagers became our home. Two young families with babies occupied one room each, and we had the small kitchen. Our possessions shrank even more. A double bed for all of us, a small table, a stove, and a cabinet were all we had.

The smudged window, which faced another old building, became my favorite spot. Sitting at it, I could turn my back on our room and on our troubled world. I pretended my parents were not hungry and frightened and could still protect and defend us. My little brother and sister had enough food to eat and space to play. There were no arrests, beatings, deportations. In the world of my imagination, everything returned to normal again, the way it had been, the way it should be. I found I could not let go of my illusions and kept returning to the window.

* * *

But my fantasies didn't fully succeed. I couldn't ignore the German night patrols marching through the silent streets. The sound of their heavy boots spread fear wherever they went. And, of course, it was impossible to ignore Herr *Leutnant* Wilm. Everyone feared him. The minute the word got out that the tall Gestapo man, in his shiny black boots, with his leather whip and the vicious dog, entered the ghetto, the streets cleared fast.

One afternoon while walking a narrow street, I heard some shouting and saw everyone run. I knew what it meant and began to run also. Within minutes, I heard barking and panting. The German shepherd! The officer had just let him loose. The dog was trained to attack, bite and leave deep wounds. Children, not able to run fast enough, often became his victims. I knew the dog ran right behind me; I could even feel his hot breath. If I continued to run straight ahead, he would get me any second. I took a sharp right turn. The dog did not. . . . The pained outcry of a little boy pierced my ears.

*   *   *

About the same time, food became more and more scarce in the ghetto, and hunger took over. I tried not to look at the begging children with spindly arms and legs, hollow cheeks, and sad, sunken eyes. I avoided the sidewalks when a dying or a dead person had been left. The bread lines grew longer and the rations smaller. Mother's once rich soup became watery, the portions skimpy. Secretly she gave us her food rations, and she grew thinner and thinner.

I still feel guilty when I think of one shameful evening. Late that night, after everyone had fallen asleep, I remained awake, reading Zola's *Nana*. I became hungry. I knew the bread was long gone, but I had seen Mother bring our weekly sugar ration earlier that day. Almost a cupful sat in a small, folded bag behind the dishes. I tiptoed to the cupboard, slowly opened the paper bag and immersed a teaspoon into the glittering pile. I planned to take only half a teaspoon, then another one, then only one more. I couldn't stop. I must have eaten half of the sugar. The next morning, Mother didn't say a word.

*   *   *

I went hungry many times and got to know the symptoms quite well. It would begin with a pleasant appetite and the anticipation of any of Mother's meals. Often *cholent*, my favorite Shabbat dinner, which I hadn't eaten since the war broke out, came to mind. *Cholent*, a complete meal in one pot, was special in many ways. The pot with all the ingredients left the house on Friday and returned on Saturday. Since Jews considered starting a fire on Shabbat sinful and our coal stoves would not stay hot through the night, *cholent* could not stay at home.

I loved to watch Mother prepare this meal. She took our largest and best pot and filled it with potatoes, whole or grated, beans, white or brown, barley soaked the night before, or coarse *kasha* (buckwheat). The meat—either beef, veal, or chicken—was added with lots of onion and garlic. Mother generously applied salt, pepper, bay leaves, and *schmaltz* (rendered chicken fat). When not in a hurry, Mother would squeeze a small glass container of *tzymes* between the meat and potatoes. *Tzymes* was the dessert, a very important part of the meal. My favorite one consisted of young carrots, raisins, brown sugar, and cinnamon. I watched Mother place a tight-fitting lid on top the pot, wrap it carefully in paper, mostly old newspapers, and tie it securely with string. In large letters she wrote our name on the paper.

A steady stream of mothers with their children hurried to the bakery before sunset. When I became older, I was given this important job. I had to walk fast enough not to miss the deadline but not so fast that I spilled the liquid or dropped the pot. We went to Mr. Greenberg's bakery, one of many Jewish bakeries in town and the one closest to our home. He delivered his freshly baked bread and rolls to our door every morning.

Friday afternoon was a busy time at the bakery. The last Shabbat *hallas* (special white bread, some with poppy seeds on top) cooled on racks, but the cakes filled with apples or plums, still came out of the oven. I could smell them blocks away. I put our *cholent* next to all the others on the floor. Since it was forbidden to pass money on Shabbat, I paid the baker right away.

I don't remember Mr. Greenberg as well as his shovel. It had a long thin wooden handle, made dark and smooth from the heat, and a flat wide blade. The elderly baker would pick up the pots, one by one, and with a graceful swing raised them high. He then carefully brought them close to the oven and slide them into the cavernous space with the glowing red coals in the back. The baker's gliding shovel reminded me of a graceful bird in flight. When the last *cholent* had been placed in the oven, he shut the heavy iron door, locked the bakery and left.

On Saturday, around 1:00 P.M. when the *Shtibels* most families attended had finished their services, droves of women and kids descended on the bakery. Everybody shoved and pushed, looking for their *cholent*. This was not so easy. The wrapping paper, darkened from prolonged heat, often became difficult to read; printed names melted into brown paper. When I found and lifted our pot, I could tell how our *cholent* had turned out. If the pot felt heavy, the *cholent* would be underdone and soggy, if too light, it had overcooked or burned. Regardless, no corrections possible.

Because of the tantalizing aroma, the walk home always seemed long. Once the pot had been placed on the table, my sister, brother, and I stood on our tiptoes to peer inside. Mother untied the string and removed the crinkled wrapping paper. As she lifted the lid, hot, savory steam hit our faces. The *cholent* was perfect. And if she had had time to prepare the small pot, then we had a real feast, a meal with a built in dessert. The pieces of meat had become tender and juicy, the small browned potatoes soft, and the barley fluffy. The onions and garlic had almost melted except for their strong aroma. The slow, almost twenty-four hours of cooking in the bakery oven did the job.

We ate right away. Mother knew everyone's preference. Father loved meat, no matter what kind, as long as it was well done and spicy; Helka was a good eater, easy to please, and I didn't pay attention to my little brother. My portion Mother made light on the meat but generous on the small browned potatoes, fluffy barley, and on the *tzymes*. Mother, of course, ate what the rest of us didn't like. I always had seconds of the glistening carrots with raisins soaked in the melted brown sugar and cinnamon. I felt sorry for the gentile kids in our neighborhood.

Occasionally, we would have an unexpected surprise. I brought home the wrong *cholent*. Mother noticed right away, but we could do nothing about it. It felt spooky to open a strange family's pot. The food looked and tasted different. We ate it anyway. Frankly, I enjoyed the occasional mix-ups.

* * *

The great food of the Passover *Seder* (a traditional festive dinner) also haunts me. Once a year, in March or April, our extended family would gather at the grandparent's home. Every one came: Father's oldest sister, Felicia, her husband, Moshe, and their four children; Chava and Felix (married with one child each); Motek, and Rifka, who lived nearby and always arrived first. Motek, about five years older than I, handsome and popular with the girls, showed interest in my reading. He once saw me carry a heavy library book on human sexuality, a forbidden topic for me. He asked my age and cautiously approved. This must have been at the time when my breasts had begun to grow. At first, a little embarrassed by them, I soon wanted the whole world to know, and I found a way. When approaching someone in the street, instead of walking towards him or her, I would run. My tiny breasts would bounce up and down. I still remember the day Father hurt my feelings. He overheard me nag Mother for my first bra while he read the paper. He raised his head and said, "A bra? What will she put in it?"

Father's only brother, Henoch, his wife, their children, two girls and a boy (almost the same ages as the three of us), also attended Passover *Seder*. Father and Uncle Henoch, both in the coal business, became competitors, and the two wives never cared for each other. Helka and I rarely saw these cousins.

After the war, when I learned that none of them had survived, I felt bad about our previous distance. Aunt Yadzia, Father's sister; Uncle Sam; their daughters Sara and Hanka—they were my favorites, and we saw them a lot. Two unmarried aunts, Sophia and Sally, lived with the grandparents and helped prepare the feast.

When the women placed the crunchy chopped liver, gefilte fish, golden chicken soup with fluffy matzo balls, and roasted goose on the table, the aroma made me hungry, but we had to wait. Grandfather conducted the *Seder* with a strict order. First the youngest child asked the Four Questions about the history and meaning of Passover. Then Grandpa took his time telling the story how Moses rescued the Jews from Egyptian slavery three thousand years before.

By the time he added the prayers and songs, the younger cousins had fallen sound asleep under the table. Our family left for home around two o'clock in the morning.

Vivid pictures of all the wonderful food I remembered danced in front of my eyes. I could smell it. I could taste it. I took my time caressing it in my mouth. Suddenly a sharp hunger pain wiped the images. I knew what came next. A throbbing headache and shimmering zigzagging lines distorted my vision. Weakness and apathy would complete the cycle. I knew the sequence well.

7

typhus epidemic broke out. The ghetto had become a perfect breeding place for disease—undernourished people living in cramped quarters, with no showers or bathtubs. Even soap had become scarce. Typhus was quite different from typhoid fever, a much milder summer sickness, which most of us had had. Typhus threatened lives. And, of course we had no medication for it. It lasted several weeks, caused a very high fever and a rash over most of the body. Lice—not the head lice or the lice of the pubic hair, eyebrows, and eyelashes, but the body lice—transmitted it. Body lice lived and laid their eggs in the seams of clothing.

Every night before going to bed, I searched for them. I turned my clothes inside out and hunted them. They often grew round and plump, and I could see my blood through their transparent skin. They left sore spots all over my body and caused intense itching and scratching. I would get rid of them only to find more the next evening. I expected to get sick any day. We all rejoiced when the ill and delirious Aunt Yadzia pulled through. Highly contagious, typhus caused many deaths. I heard the frightening bell of the horse-drawn ambulance more and more often. Patients were taken to the hospital, frequently against their will, and the families kept under strict quarantine.

Young men of the Sanitary Service carried out a ghoulish job. One of them was Richard. His mother, a young widow, and his two brothers moved into our ghetto. I liked him right away. There was something about him. He had a warm smile and treated the sick he transported in the simple ambulance kindly. And, of course, he was handsome. We had common friends but no close contact, and anyway, he had a girlfriend. I was petrified when he came down with the typhus. Friends kept me informed about the progress of his illness, and I rejoiced when I heard he made it. I kept thinking about him, even after I escaped from Piotrkow.

*   *   *

By late 1941, nothing had improved. Arrests and deportations became common. One time, in the middle of the night, two Jewish policemen, the ones who carried out German orders, came for Father. They ordered him out of bed. The tall man seemed fidgety. "Hurry up," he said. "What takes you so long? Do you think you are the only one? We have more places to go."

As Father struggled with his pants, I felt embarrassed that the strangers saw him in his underwear. His hands shook as he tried to button his sweater. They did not answer Mother's repeated questions or give any explanation for their actions. As they took him away, Father tried to smile at us. "Go back to sleep," he said. "I'll be fine. I'll be back tomorrow."

My eyes wet, I watched the men take Father out of the door. Only little Natek fell asleep again. Most arrested men were sent to unknown destinations, supposedly to some job. Frequently, it wasn't work at all, and they never came back. The Germans beat the ones who did return. The next day, Father did come back, and I could see no signs of beating.

*   *   *

After the arrest in the middle of the night, it was obvious that Father had to have a job the Germans considered essential to their "war effort." These jobs were very hard to get. Mother took care of that. She illegally left the ghetto and approached Mr. Kopydlowski, a Pole and owner of a lumberyard. Before the war, he had been one of our customers. After Mother pleaded with him to save Father, he promised to hire him. Father, with other Jews who worked there, carried heavy boards and loaded them onto trucks. Because the Germans needed the wood, the job gave Father temporary security from arrest and deportation. Neither Mother, my sister, nor I were able to find any work. We remained unprotected in spite of Uncle Sam's efforts.

Uncle Sam, Hanka and Sara's father, was a respected member of the Jewish Council, which the Germans formed early in the occupation. It consisted of a group of Jews, politically active before the war, or who were prominent and well known in the community.

The Germans passed all their demands to the Jewish Council and expected total compliance. Not an easy task. Each member had charge of a separate department. Uncle Sam's responsibility encompassed the Jewish work force. His job was to deliver, frequently on a short notice, any number of Jewish men the Germans demanded. Everyone feared his calls. Wealthy families tried to protect their men with money. But, Uncle Sam's answer remained the same: "The poor men are as important as the rich ones." He was honest, fair and refused to take bribes. He fell under constant pressure both from the Jewish community and the Germans and was not at all the man I remembered.

My memory from before the war of Uncle Sam, who was always attentive to his appearance and his tailor business, was that he had a great voice and liked to sing while working. He had trained with Grandfather where he met and fell in love with the petite and pretty Aunt Yadzia. They got married in spite of Grandfather's objections. Uncle Sam did not fit too well into the family: He wasn't religious, but he was an active socialist and a performer in the amateur theater. He socialized easily and had many friends. When Helka and I visited, cheerful Aunt Yadzia gladly gave us seconds of her famous cake. It had sweet crumbs on top, and she kept it in the bedroom.

I looked up to and was somewhat intimidated by Cousin Sara, the attractive teenager with her sophisticated friends. The young men and women who often filled her home paid no attention to me. I also admired her business school diploma and stylish clothes.

8

In the summer of 1942, almost three years after the Germans forced my family into the ghetto, where hunger, typhus, arrests, and deportations increased in regularity, I began to hear rumors of "liquidations." The Germans seemed to be following a certain order in eliminating one ghetto after another. Such liquidations seemed to be getting closer. Everyone's mood plummeted. Except for a few men and women with jobs considered necessary for the German war effort, the rest of us felt trapped. The word Treblinka came up. A young man had escaped and repeated what he had learned: cattle cars, poison gas, big ovens. I heard the chilling news everywhere.

Only Grandfather remained calm. He did not believe it. "It's a lie, a big lie!" he would shout in anger. "God will not allow it!"

I envied my grandfather's faith, but I did believe. I was nineteen, and I did not want to die. I especially did not want to be killed by the Germans. I kept nagging my mother: "Why don't we do something?"

"Please leave me alone," she pleaded. "What will happen to others will happen to us."

But I wouldn't leave her alone, wouldn't stop nagging her. There had to be something to do. One day, halfheartedly Mother said, "If Danka gave you her ID card . . ." She didn't have to say more.

* * *

A few days later, I heard a soft knock on the door. I opened it. Danka and Mala! They had come! Even with their church across the street, with the front door facing the Polish side and the back facing the ghetto, making it possible for them to sneak in and out, no one had done it. The penalty was death on the spot for Jews, most likely for Poles as well.

My friends stepped in and quickly shut the door. Their eyes went back and forth: the cramped room and the five of us. No words. So, our friendship still lived. I saw my first glimmer of hope in a long time.

Mother was the first to speak. She talked about the looming disaster of liquidation and cautiously brought up the subject of Danka's ID card. The girls listened.

"We have to talk to our mother," said Danka. "We'll be back."

And they left. The silence hung over the room for the longest time. I almost began to believe their presence had been a mirage. I was sure Mrs. Justyna, the girls' mother, would never agree. Rumors of impending liquidation intensified. Panic grew.

Shortly afterwards the girls returned. "Pick a name, paste on a photo and sign it." They handed over three IDs, for Mother, Helka, and me.

I remember the look my parents exchanged . . . total disbelief.

* * *

Our situation had changed dramatically. Father had a secure job, Natek was too young to need an ID, and Mother, Helka, and I had false papers.

"Choose different last names. It might be safer not to be related," said Mother.

I began to worry if my Aryan looks were good enough to pass for a Polish girl. Danka suggested I bleach my hair, but Mother felt I shouldn't. "It could be conspicuous," she said, "even dangerous if it showed. Anyway, not all Poles are blond." As few women colored their hair at that time; someone might get suspicious noticing dark roots.

After smudging the IDs to make them look used, Mother hid them in a drawer between some underwear. We waited.

News of the liquidation scared me, but so did the plan to escape. We risked death either way. In the next few days, that fear didn't leave. I hardly dared to look at the small documents with the stamps and the signatures. I wondered if it was possible to be a Pole on the outside and a Jew inside. So many things could easily give me away. Anyone could tell that I was sad, cautious and frightened. On that alone, I might be arrested and delivered to the Gestapo. It had happened to many others. I almost believed the risk was greater if I tried. I might as well forget the false papers.

Mother kept repeating, "The looks aren't everything. You speak accent-free Polish and know the Catholic religion. Stop worrying."

My doubts persisted.

* * *

One evening, shortly before curfew, as I was rushing through the deserted streets, I ran into Julius, the friend in whose apartment our book group used to meet. That seemed a lifetime ago; we were all too scared to read now. Now it was a matter of life or death. We all feared the ghetto had only a few days left.

Even though I hadn't seen Julius for a long time, I shared with him my secret. I had a false Polish ID, hidden in a drawer. Then I told him I had lost my courage; I was afraid they would recognize me and didn't want to use it. When he heard that, he raised his voice in anger. "Don't you dare talk like that," he said, "I'm a circumcised Jew, but if I had a false ID, I wouldn't hesitate for a minute to try to escape the ghetto."

I knew that no other men in Poland were circumcised. A simple exam and he would be easily discovered. Yet he would use an ID if he had one. That refocused my thinking. I realized how lucky I was. False IDs were extremely expensive and almost impossible to get. I had one, and I was considering wasting it. Only a short time before, I had nagged my mother to do something, because I didn't want to die. I felt ashamed. I was ready to use the small piece of paper to stay alive. If it wasn't for Julius . . .

9

Midnight on October 14, 1942. The arrival of a neighbor from upstairs broke the silence of our apartment building. Returning from work, he had just come from the train station.

"They're here, the *Sonder Kommando* [the Special Commando] and their helpers—the East Europeans!" he shouted. "They're at the station, still unloading."

In my mind, I could see our small, poorly lit train station. Instead of the muffled activities typical at this time of night, the place was brightly lit and busting with noise and commotion. Laughter, loud voices, and the barking dogs resonated for blocks. Everyone knew well what it meant. They had come to liquidate our ghetto.

The Market Square "selections" came first. They forced every man, woman, and child to walk in front of a Gestapo officer. After a quick inspection, he would decide who went to the right, who went to the left. They would keep a small group of young, strong men and women for slave labor. The armed Nazis, their helpers, and the frightening dogs would lead the rest of the people to the railroad station. They would pack them into the waiting cattle cars and send them off to the gas chambers in Treblinka.

The loud, agitated voice of our neighbor woke up the tenants. The half-asleep men and women, in their nightgowns or long underwear, didn't care about their missing dentures or disheveled hair as they tumbled into the hall to listen to him. As the man repeated the news, someone shouted, "Are you sure they weren't ordinary soldiers? How could you tell in the dark?" "How many of them were there?" asked a woman. A husky man, a few steps down, threw up his arm and said, "That's all nonsense. Its just another Gestapo unit. They constantly come and go. I also work at the station. I've seen them many times."

The neighbor who brought the news looked stunned. They didn't believe him; they still had hope. He shook his head and, with a deep sigh, climbed the steps to his apartment.

Relieved, the families began returning to their cramped apartments. We followed the young mother as she hugged her two-year-old boy and sobbed quietly. Father locked the door, and we listened. When it got quiet, he whispered, "We are leaving right now."

I put on extra clothes: double underwear, a skirt with two tops, and the winter coat. We didn't have much more than that by then. I took off and tossed aside the white armband with the blue Star of David. Mother handed false papers to Helka and me. Then we walked out. A tall black pot with Mother's vegetable-oatmeal soup was sitting on the stove.

The building remained dark as we crept down the steps. Our destination—Mr. Kopydlowski's lumberyard, Father's work place, only few blocks away. Escape wasn't far, but it was terrifying. Only Father had left the ghetto in the last three years. Discovered, we faced death on the spot.

Father looked around. No guard in sight. "Let's go!" he husked.

One by one, we came out of the building and took a sharp left turn. In only a few steps, we had left the ghetto. My eyes darted about me, looking at the centuries-old Catholic church, then the dark windows of our dilapidated building. The street lay silent, empty and dark.

"Let's split up," said Father. "Mother and Natek in the front, Sabka and Helka half a block behind. I will be in the back."

We stayed close to the buildings to be able to dash into an entrance if needed. We walked briskly but stepped quietly on the cobblestones. As we approached the corner, I felt sure someone watched us. No one was there.

The lumberyard was closed—dark, quiet and empty. Father led us to a remote corner, where the five of us huddled on a stack of boards. I dozed only to startle awake, then doze off and wake again.

A couple of hours later, noise pierced the stillness of the night. Motorcycles, cars, and trucks stopped with loud screeches to unload shouting men and barking dogs. The *Sonder Kommando . . .* they were surrounding the ghetto. The liquidation wasn't rumor any more. The end had come for the Piotrkow Jews.

* * *

We huddled outside the trap, but we didn't know what to do next. Only Father could remain in the lumberyard. The four of us: Mother, our little brother, my sister, and I would have to leave . . . and soon before the Polish workers arrived.

We had no plan. Our parents decided the four of us shouldn't stay together—too dangerous. Mother would be with Natek, and I with Helka. We hoped the Polish friends and neighbors we could trust would give us shelter for a few days. Once the Special Commander liquidated our ghetto and moved to the next town, we would try to join up again. "As long as the five of us are together." I had heard Mother say it over and over again. Strength lay in numbers, but not now.

Father didn't say much. He kissed each of us, his eyes full of fear. The day had not yet broken when we left him.

10

After leaving the lumberyard, we separated right away. I don't remember where Mother and Natek went, but she told Helka and me to approach Mrs. Justyna, Danka and Mala's mother.

It didn't take us long to pass through the once familiar streets. We quickly reached the large, modern home with the apple orchard just outside the city. The nearby park and the open fields made it secluded. After some hesitation, I knocked on the door. When Mrs. Justyna saw Helka and me, she was shocked but didn't ask any questions. She ushered us in quickly, gave us some food and sent Danka, Mala, and the two of us to the shed in the orchard. The small wooden shed, set close to the house, had two benches and sacks of apples, potatoes, and cabbages that took up most of the dirt floor. Helka and I clung to each other on one of the benches wrapped in a coarse blanket. A cold wind blew through the cracks in the wall. We were only a few kilometers from the ghetto. We could hear gunshots and piercing cries and screams. The children's outcries cut the worse. It all seemed so close. The night dragged on. It frightened Mrs. Justyna, and the next morning we had to leave.

* * *

The first day, Helka and I spent on our own, was scary. We didn't know what to do or where to go. By midmorning, we began to wander around.

The Polish part of town, where we grew up and which we loved, had become illegal and dangerous. Everything seemed strange. The streets looked wide, clean, sparsely populated, and the people looked well nourished and well dressed. No frightened looks as in the ghetto. We tried to imitate the Poles' confident manner. We walked briskly as if with a purpose. We avoided our old neighborhood so as not to be recognized. The glances of the people we passed began to worry me. We left for the outskirts of town and found a large open field. We walked back and forth, back and forth . . . all day long. We tried to sit for a while so as not to be so visible, but the ground was cold and damp and left dark spots on our coats.

The days that followed didn't improve. Most of our previous customers and neighbors were afraid to keep us. A hot meal or a one-night stay was all anyone offered. We lived from day to day, actually from hour to hour. The decisions we had to make on the spur of the moment rarely improved our situation. The echoing gun shots and the screams from the ghetto didn't let up. "What do we do next?" Helka asked me and I asked her. Our situation seemed to be hopeless, but I wasn't ready to give up.

Sometimes we were lucky. All Saints' Day, a widely observed Catholic holiday, turned out to be a boon for us. We spent the whole day at the cemetery among other Poles, pretending to visit a grave of someone dear. We looked for a neglected, out-of-the-way grave with no headstone or name. The relatives were less likely to show up; we planned to claim a mix-up if they did. Each of us picked a grave, and we worked to bring it back to the original condition. With great care, I would straighten leaning wooden crosses, remove fallen leaves, pull weeds, and line up the stones around the edges. When we finished the job on a grave, we knelt, crossed ourselves and pretended to pray. In the course of the day, we restored several graves.

A couple of days later we nearly met disaster. Helka and I were walking aimlessly along a quiet street. As we turned the corner, a young Polish policeman faced us. I could feel that my face turned beet red and my fright could be seen. He gave us a long look as he passed. I expected him to turn around, ask questions and take us to the Gestapo. He kept walking.

* * *

Night shelters became harder to find. One evening we decided to approach a once-friendly customer from our father's coal business. It was already pitch dark when we knocked on the door. When the lady answered and saw the two of us, she . . . gasped. Avoiding our eyes, she began politely to turn us down. Bolek, her teenage son, our childhood playmate, with whom we used to spend a lot of time, came also to the door. His look was not friendly. After a few minutes, without a word, he took his jacket and went out. Helka and I left in a hurry. The only place to hide was an apartment building nearby. We ran to the top of the stairway and pressed into a dark corner. I kept listening for the boy and a policeman. It took a long time for my fear to lift.

* * *

Shortly afterwards came another night with no place to go. Again we headed for the top floor of an unfamiliar apartment building. Three doors faced us on the dark stairway. The aroma of a roasted chicken came from the middle door. "I'm hungry," whimpered Helka. "When will we get some food?"

"Hush now, they might hear us."

The laughing children in the first apartment and the quarreling adults next door kept me on edge. What if someone burst out? But slowly the noises died down, and silence filled the cold stairway. Leaning against the wall, I moved close to Helka, wrapped the coat around me and began to doze.

Suddenly, I had to urinate. At first, I thought I could hold it, but I couldn't. A steady stream of urine cascaded from step to step. The sound petrified us. A puddle formed in front of the entrance door.

* * *

Since Mother and Natek and my sister and I separated from Father in the lumber yard, our contact had become erratic. Natek, then eleven, became the messenger. In spite of the danger, he crossed the town alone several times. Our parents desperately tried to keep in touch and make some plans. Now, that the *Sonder Kommando* had finished off the Piotrkow ghetto, Father hoped to find jobs for us so we could be together again. He found nothing.

Meanwhile, the four of us had hardly managed to see each other. Each day became more unpredictable. I remember seeing Mother only once. She had aged a lot in just a few days. Her gray hair had lost its luster, her face looked haggard. I noticed that she had put her best shoes, the black pumps, on the wrong feet.

"It's not a mistake," she said. "They got wet and stretched. They kept falling off."

* * *

Finding places for Helka and me to hide steadily became more and more difficult. One evening, ignoring the danger of being recognized, we went to the apartment building in which we used to live. Mrs. Kropla, Mother's favorite neighbor, still lived on the main floor. Spunky, hard-working and a widow with two grown children, she had a small grocery store next to her apartment. Mother used to send Helka or me to buy the delicious, but forbidden, Polish sausages, which we hid from our Jewish neighbors.

I was to blame for this transgression. A few years before, in the playground of my grade school, a girl accidentally hit me in the back. I began to cough and spit up some blood. Mother panicked, sure I had TB. Even though the doctor didn't find it, he felt I was skinny—a known risk factor for that disease—and asked if Mother would allow me to eat ham. It would help me gain weight. Mother didn't hesitate, and the non-kosher sausage entered our home. I was glad. While Mother worried about TB, I worried about finding a boy friend. Ever since I heard Father say: "Mrs. Stern [our customer] is so skinny she looks like a long spaghetti. I didn't think she would ever find a husband."

Slender women were not considered feminine.

Mrs. Kropla knew about our sausage secret and used to wink and smile when she handed us the package. Now she gave us a hot meal and let us stay through the night. As she reached for the round, crusty bread and the red beet jam (no fruit available), she said: "Wasn't it terrible about your mother?"

A knot formed in my stomach. "What happened?" we both cried out.

"Oh," she said, her eyes avoiding us. "I hate to be the one to tell you, but a few days ago they brought your mother to the police station."

Apparently as Natek brought her a message from our father, a few Polish boys recognized him and began to chase him shouting: "Jew! Jew!" Soon a large crowd followed him. In the commotion, Mother whispered to him "Run!" He escaped, and she was arrested.

"I'm sorry," said Mrs. Kropla. She didn't have to say any more. I knew what would come next. I had heard it before. They would take her to the large synagogue already full of other Jews caught in hiding. The Germans and their Ukrainian helpers kept adding more men, women and children. The despair and stench must have been unbearable. In a few days, they would lock her in a cattle car and send her to Treblinka. I knew all of this, and yet I couldn't stop eating the dark bread with the beet jam.

Mother at the beginning of the war.

11

The next day dawned to a new reality. Mother was gone. Despite her distinguished Aryan looks and accent-free Polish, they had recognized her and delivered her to the Gestapo. The hope for the five of us to be together again had evaporated. Natek had run back to our father, who was able to include him in his work. My sister and I had no place to hide.

We decided to try Mrs. Justyna again. This time she didn't have the heart to turn us away. Apparently, Mother had come a few days earlier and on her knees begged her to give shelter to Helka and me, reminding her of her dead son, Yourek.

He had been about four years older than Danka and played with us in the park across the street from our coal yard. He had epilepsy, which, at that time, had no treatment, no medication. As a devoted Catholic, Mrs. Justyna took her small boy on a pilgrimage to Chestochowa. There, at the Catholic shrine of the Black Madonna, the most holy place in Poland, she prayed for a miracle. No miracle happened. Yourek kept getting epileptic attacks, and his behavior became unpredictable; he required constant supervision. As a tall, strong teenager, he often became sexually aroused. He would wet his lips and run after strange girls shouting: "Let's kiss! Let's kiss!" When the young nanny couldn't handle him, our mother took over. After a seizure, my parents would bring him to the coal yard, and Mother watched over him. Mrs. Justyna, away at work, knew she could rely on my mother. She remembered it well.

She put us up in the attic. I knew nothing about the attic. I was familiar with the orchard and the spacious house from when it was being built a few
years before the war. The four of us used to play outdoors, getting in the way
of the workers. Helka once fell in a pit full of lime and had to be quickly
scrubbed clean.

Danka and Mala pulled out a ladder and climbed up with us. A dark,
cramped space, filled with broken furniture, bags and boxes, dust covered
everything—a perfect place for bats. Little more than a crawl space really, with
the ceiling so low, we couldn't stand up but had to sit or lie down. Two pillows
and some old blankets kept us warm. The tiny window facing the street
became our only connection with the outside world. I never edged close to it.
It wasn't safe. A narrow beam of light would sneak in during the day and a star
would twinkle at me at night. The sound of whistling wind or pelting rain
would break the long, monotonous hours. The day stretched endlessly. Still, I
didn't mind. I loved the attic. I would listen to the outside world, but I didn't
miss it. The outside world wasn't good to us. The aimless walks in the naked
fields and the scary nights in open stairways—I was glad to put them behind us.
No more suspicious strangers or old neighbors I couldn't trust any more.

In the long hours of darkness and silence, when Helka and I hardly
spoke to each other, Mother's image filled my head. I could see a screaming
mob, policemen, Natek out of breath, and Mother. They stood, pale and

The Justyna house. Note the small attic window. We hid up there.

50

frightened, while the onlookers pushed and shoved. It didn't take long. As they led her away, her eyes followed her little boy running, running fast.

They took her to the large synagogue—it was not large anymore—packed with people. People caught like her. Jews. Our neighbors, friends, maybe other members of our family. Some shouted and cried. Some prayed. Others seemed lost. Mother must have worried about Natek, Helka, and me. Each time the door opened and the Germans shoved in more men, women, and children, Mother would call our names.

Some people must have died in the crowded synagogue. If she made it to the cattle car, it was too late; these doors were sealed. I pictured her looking ashen, her lips dry and cracked from thirst.

If she was still alive when the train reached Treblinka, her eyes would be glazed and vacant. She let them push her along with the crowd into the gas chambers. Where did my mother die? There was no one to tell me.

* * *

The downstairs door opened with a loud squeak. Mr. Justyna had returned. A biology professor, he was introverted and cautious. He didn't know we huddled in the attic. He would never have allowed us to enter his house. Because we lay right above the kitchen, we had to be absolutely quiet. I kept worrying about an unexpected sneeze or cough. In the morning, after Mr. Justyna left the house, Helka and I came down, straightened our stiff backs and ate with Mrs. Justyna and the girls.

It felt so good to be down in the large warm kitchen full of light. Outside, the almost naked trees swayed gently, and the dry leaves rustled under the feet of the playful dog. The fried eggs sizzled and the vegetable soup bubbled on the hot coal stove. It seemed so normal. The whole world seemed normal again.

But, that ended quickly. Mrs. Justyna had heard rumors that frightened her. We had to leave.

I still remember the farewell. Her voice quavered, and she was visibly distraught when she gave us the news.

"My dear girls, I'm sorry that I have to send you off, but I know that *Jesus Christus* will watch over you and protect you." She made the sign of the cross on our foreheads, hugged and kissed us and hung a religious medallion on Helka's and my neck. "Danusia and Mala, please walk with them."

She gave each of us a small prayer book, some food, and left quickly.

"Where should we go now?" Helka said. "There's no place for us. It's hopeless. What's the use, they will get us for sure."

Unless we listened to Father.

I don't recall how we got the message, but Father had a plan. We should go to Germany as volunteer workers. We were to apply in an employment office but not one in our city. Someone could recognize us. What happened to Mother could happen to the two of us. Father directed us to walk on foot to another town, apply for work and leave from there. Father kept worrying about us.

The thought of going into Germany, the country of our enemies terrified us. But Father had an explanation.

By the end of 1942, the German military successes had flagged. The Russian front demanded more and more soldiers and equipment. The German workforce back home had been badly depleted, and they needed new workers. The German government was bringing them in—mostly by force—from occupied countries. By that time, Germany probably had millions of foreigners within its borders, and they couldn't tell them apart. It might be safer for a Jew to be there than in Poland. Father knew this.

November. Blustery and cold. Nights would be colder. We put on extra clothes and checked the small amount of money Mother had sewn into our bras. Danka and Mala walked with us to the outskirts of town. The rest of the way, we walked alone, briskly, on the side roads.

As we reached Radomsko, a small town near Piotrkow, and we stood in front of the employment office, a sudden fear overtook me. We had escaped the ghetto two hours before the liquidation began. In the Polish part of town, only a few old customers and neighbors dared to give us shelter. Most of the time, we had spent in open fields, the cemetery, stairways, and the attic. Now, even that had come to an end.

We had to step into the open. The false papers, held unused in our pockets, had to become our real papers. We had to look and act like Polish girls. We should not have fear or sadness in our eyes. As I looked at the building, I had no idea who I would find behind the doors. Certainly, it might be

German officers, but it could also be Polish police. If they asked questions, we would have to have answers. If they become suspicious, we could be facing our end. I kept staring at the run-down building.

"Both of us don't have to go in. Why don't I go first?" said Helka, my brave little sister.

"Are you sure? What will you say? Just ask about work in Germany and look him straight in the eyes."

"Yes, yes, I know. Don't worry." And she left.

I watched her go up the steps. Images of Mother being arrested came to my mind. I paced back and forth on the sidewalk across the street. Minutes expanded into an eternity. I panicked at the idea that she might not come out. Then guilt set in. I should have been the one to go in. I was the oldest. I should have taken the risk. I should have been the one. But . . . Helka came out. She stood in front of the door and waved at me.

The office wasn't threatening at all. A middle-aged, mild-mannered and somewhat bored-looking Polish man, he sat alone behind a large desk, carefully checking our papers. He looked at the photos, the stamps, and the signatures. They seemed okay, but then he began to wonder out loud: "Since you live in Piotrkow, a much larger city with its own employment office, why did you come to Radomsko to volunteer?"

I hadn't expected that question.

"Well," I said with a forced smile, "we've been staying here with our aunt. Once we decided to work in Germany, she suggested not to bother going back."

It made sense to him. He gave us back our papers.

12

Our next destination became the large transit center in Czestochowa from where every man and woman—volunteer or not—was transported to Germany. When we arrived at the large, sprawling, compound, hundreds of future workers milled around. They arrived daily from many towns and villages. Trucks brought them in, and trains would take them away.

I could easily tell the volunteers from the forced workers. They were the cheerful ones; they left of their own free will. The forced workers, frequently snatched off the streets in their hometowns, looked subdued. With painful separations still fresh, they dreaded the prospect of living and working in hostile Germany.

The transit center was run by German and Polish officials. It took about a week to go through the clearing process. First they checked the documents. We stood in line for a long time. When I finally reached the table, the person in charge opened up my small ID booklet, breezed through all the data, closed it, and gave it back to me. She hardly looked at the photo or me. I had worried the entire time we had spent in the line for nothing.

Delousing came next. This proved to be the worst part of the experience. Large groups of naked women were ushered into open showers. The water was hot, the soap strong, and it smelled obnoxious. They sprinkled the coarse DDT powder on our hair, bodies, and clothes, the clothes we wore, as well as the clothes in the suitcases or bundles. It felt degrading. It also conjured up a frightening parallel. Naked women herded into showers with chemicals. The concentration camps. Chemicals there killed Jews; here they killed lice.

With hundreds of people to be checked, the process crawled. The compound teamed with young men and women waiting for the next test. We tried to blend in, but it wasn't easy. Our pre-war self-confidence with the Poles had been markedly reduced. The three-year separation in the ghetto did that. But staying by ourselves wasn't good either. It might raise suspicion. We would join a group, listen to the conversation, add a word or two and move on. Only superficial contact seemed safe.

I watched for suspicious looks and spent a lot of our free time outside the camp. We walked in the city and visited the church with the famous shrine of the Black Madonna. For centuries, it had been the most holy place for Polish Catholics. The annual pilgrimage to Chestochowa attracted many believers. Imposing on the outside, the inside of the church overwhelmed us—the tall cavernous space, the many religious ornaments, the darkness and silence. Neither the weak light rays, filtered through the stained glass windows, nor the whisper of prayers disturbed this. As Helka and I entered the church, we dipped our fingers into the holy water, crossed ourselves and knelt next to the praying men and women. We made sure they could hear our prayers. We felt safe in the church and spent long hours there.

One afternoon, as we stood in yet another endless line, this time waiting for meal tickets, a loud "Hi, Sabka. What are you doing here?" came from behind me.

I froze. It was Wladek, brother of Maria, my grade-school friend and neighbor. I had been in their home many times. I sang Christmas carols with them and exchanged our Passover matzo for their forbidden Easter cake.

He was happy to see us. I took him aside and explained our situation. We were trying to be one of them. Going to Germany was our only hope. He understood. "Why don't I sign up for the same work place. We would be together, and I could protect the two of you? "

Wladek was a likeable young man. He was popular and had already made many friends. But . . . he liked to drink. We tried to avoid him and were happy when his transport left before ours.

After nearly a week, the preparations for our departure had progressed well. Only the medical checkup remained. A friendly, young Polish doctor did the exam. He noticed the extensive redness of our skin. The body lice we had picked up in the ghetto during the typhus epidemic had done that. We still itched and scratched. The doctor, not knowing the cause of the rash, offered to exempt us. He assumed the Germans had caught us in one of their roundups and were forcing us to go to Germany. No other way would two decent-looking Polish girls be there. We didn't look like the volunteers—the poor, ignorant peasant girls from the villages or the rough ones from the big cities.

I tried to be convincing in my explanation. "The recent family situation is such that going to Germany is our best option."

He looked puzzled. I could tell my explanation didn't work. "Actually, the situation is quite bad. Our father, a cavalry officer, was drafted at the beginning of the war and never came back. Mother struggled financially and mentally. At the end of July, she had a nervous breakdown. The family separated the two of us. We were being passed from one relative to another."

The doctor's face softened. He put a stamp on our documents.

13

Finally, we boarded the train to Germany. We had made it so far, but we had no idea what lay ahead. Working and living among the Germans, the people who accepted Hitler's plan to kill every one of us, repulsed and frightened us.

From the time the war broke out, trains in occupied Europe had been full of Jews. They traveled in sealed cattle cars. Jews from Germany, France, Holland, Belgium, and other West European countries traveled east, mostly to Auschwitz—the infamous concentration camp near the Polish-German border. Trains took most Polish Jews to Treblinka, near Warsaw, and other camps with gas chambers and crematoria.

The train we boarded had no cattle cars; it was a passenger train heading west into Germany for work and, we hoped, for our survival. If we should work among Poles, we would have to be especially careful and pretend to be observant Catholics, as were most of them. Pretend, pretend. That constant need—to pretend to be what we were not—left us open to incalculable risk. Even a small mistake could give us away. It wouldn't take much: a wrong name, a wrong expression, or a Yiddish word infiltrating our speech. I didn't want to think about all the risks. I watched the naked trees glide by.

"Anyone to play cards?" A young woman headed in my direction. I turned towards the window and closed my eyes. "We need one more person." She walked past our seat.

Helka and I tried to avoid boisterous men and women. A good part of the time, we either stared out the window or kept our eyes closed. The long hours on the train made me homesick. I didn't want to be on that train. I wanted to be home with Mother and Father. I had never been away from them. The parents, whom I always considered one unit, had become separate individuals. I could see them in my mind.

My father, a tall, slender, youthful-looking man, had four sisters and a brother and was the youngest and brightest of the six children. Grandfather hoped he would become a rabbi. Father had progressed pretty far on his way to that goal when he met Sam, grandfather's apprentice. Within a short time, under Sam's influence, he became a *Bundist*—a socialist. Like all religious Jews in Poland, Father had not received a secular education. Self-educated, he

Mother (right), when she was single, and her sister Guta.

read constantly. After he married and started a family, he became a businessman. Before the war, during the Depression when it was hard to make ends meet, Mother constantly complained: "You never have time for our business; the whole world is more important to you. Newspapers, all the newspapers."

Father did love newspapers, most of them national and representing different political parties. The *Yiddish Forward* was his favorite, but he read various Polish papers as well. My sister and I loved the Saturday afternoons we occasionally spent with him. In an elegant cafe, Father would order our favorite pastries for us, hot, strong tea for himself, and reach for the newspapers he didn't have at home. Each paper came attached to a long, smooth wooden bar to keep the pages together. It hung on a special metal hook. These papers looked very important to me. Father could spend most of the day there. When Helka and I had had enough, we would play in the park nearby or go home.

I also loved the Sunday mornings when Father read to us the latest news. Ever since Hitler came to power in 1933, he watched the creation of the

Nazi Party and the powerful military establishment. Hitler persecuted his opponents and appealed to the German people. The majority believed in him and gladly followed, while the skeptical minority grew frightened and fell silent. Hitler had a quick fix for the economic and psychological depression after Germany's defeat in the First World War. He focused on Jews—the customary scapegoat. Jews were the problem, he told the people, and he had the solution. He turned his attention first on the assimilated, patriotic German Jews. The Third Reich stripped them of their businesses and professional jobs. It sent them to concentration camps, where most of them perished. Some of these Jews could not bear their country's betrayal and committed suicide.

One story remains vivid in my mind. The Germans arrested a young Jewish man in Berlin and, together with others, led him to an unknown destination. The armed Nazis marched them at a quick pace. The man's right shoelace came undone. He couldn't decide whether to stop and tie it or keep walking with a loose, flapping shoe. He feared the loose shoe would slow him down, but he didn't dare stop to tie it. I never found out what happened.

Our parents met in Piotrkow in 1921 when Mother came from Warsaw to teach. She was born and raised in Lukow, a small town nearby. Her father, once a wealthy landowner, and the family spent a lot of time in the country. She loved animals and respected nature.

My cousin Sara remembered the impact Mother made when she arrived. Mother, about thirty-four, ten years older than Father, gray haired and distinguished looking, wore stylish clothes—slacks and a man's cap. She was intelligent and self-confident—an emancipated woman. Her college education was unusual for a woman at that time. Her favorite writer was Tolstoy, to whom she had written a letter as a teenager and received a reply. She recited Polish and Russian poetry from memory. Concerned about my education, she had encouraged me to be independent, to rely on myself. She had said it many times: "You never know what life might bring, and only your knowledge cannot be taken from you."

As a teenager, I became aware of my parents' age difference. People who didn't know us would take Mother for my grandmother and Father for my brother. I felt embarrassed. When I was born, Mother was thirty-five and Father twenty-five, a huge difference. Mother's gray hair made the difference more pronounced. My friends' mothers were either younger or the same age as their fathers.

I still remember a disquieting incident. One of Father's customers, a strange man about whom everybody made fun, became angry with Father and looked for revenge. One day, he saw me alone in the coal yard and said with a malicious smile, "I bet you couldn't guess the secret I know about you." Of course, I insisted he tell me. "You were born before the nine months were up. Heh-heh-heh-heh!" And he ran off, his long, torn garment dragging on the dusty ground.

I was angry, furious with my parents. How dare they bring such shame on me. Wasn't the age difference bad enough? This news became my deepest secret. I reached adulthood before I could talk about it.

Eventually, only among strangers did my parents' age difference matter to me. It didn't matter at home. At home, everything seemed entirely normal. Only once, when Father attended a gathering did Mother send me along with the warning, "Watch him." I don't know if she was serious. The occasional arguments, mostly about the business, passed quickly. Mother, strong willed, usually got her way; easy-going and agreeable Father gave in quickly. I remember few social friends. Most of my parents' free time they spent with Father's family, some customers, and neighbors. They seemed comfortable and content to me.

* * *

A sudden jolt of the train brought me back to reality. November 1942, and we just crossed the border into Germany. The landscape didn't change much. The bare fields, dense woods, and slowly flowing rivers looked the same as in Poland. When I realized we had reached Germany, my fears returned.

GERMANY

14

The train trip lasted several days, but I have only a vague recollection of most of it. The train stopped several times, and large and small groups debarked. Tension mounted as names were called. Newly made friendships broke, apprehension grew. Especially for the two of us.

Helka and I continued to be cautious among the boisterous men and women. Several hundred of us rode in the car at any time.

Our destination came—Neustadt/Orla. Neustadt, on the river Orla, located in Thuringen, a central state of Germany. Our names were called, and we got off the train to board a waiting truck. I could tell Neustadt was a small town when the truck drove us from the railroad station to the barracks, a nondescript building that housed women only. The building contained a huge hall with rows of bunk beds and a smaller one with long tables and benches. Hundreds of foreign women had been there for some time. They came from occupied countries all over Europe. I heard several foreign languages. Polish women, most of them young and sturdy, comprised the majority. They were happy to see the new transport and hoped to find someone from their home-towns. Loud questions and answers bounced back and forth. Helka and I pretended to share in the excitement. Luckily, no one came from Piotrkow.

Herr Uhlmann, the man in charge of the camp, checked our documents, assigned bunk beds (the two of us got to share a double-decker) and handed out meal tickets. We had to be at work on time, observe the camp curfew and wear the letter P. Only Polish men and women were required to wear this visible sign on their clothes. Germans trusted Poles the least.

The mistrust and hatred was mutual. Poland, a medium-sized country in central Europe, had borders on the east with Russia and on the west with Germany. For centuries, the two giants had repeatedly attacked and occupied Poland. Periods of independence were few and short-lived. The last period of Polish freedom had lasted from 1918, the end of the First World War, until 1939, the beginning of the Second World War. Poles remained intensely patriotic. Shortly after the 1939 German occupation in the western part of Poland (my part of the country), a wide-spread and effective underground movement had been created. The majority of the Polish population became actively involved. Germans considered the Polish people a serious threat.

Our work began the next day. Women from our transport were assigned various jobs. Herr Uhlmann decided who went where. He sent Helka and me to the *Baumaschinen Fabrik*, a factory for heavy-construction equipment. A foreman came for our small group early the next morning. He called our names and checked the IDs. He wore civilian clothes but seemed as cold and rigid as any military officer.

The factory, tucked away on the outskirts of town in a sparsely populated area, had a guard and a locked gate. The compound consisted of several buildings, some large and spacious, with a few small ones and one fairly new office building. Our work assignment: one of the large halls with several assembly lines. It was crowded, with lots of dust in the air and overwhelming noise.

I had never been in a factory before. The fast-moving machines spit out crude, bulky pieces of metal. With each short stop, these had to be trimmed, polished and given a definite shape. The workers had to be quick and precise in what they did. When the conveyor brought the round disc to my station, I had to pull a heavy lever and puncture a small hole in the center, in the exact center, of the disc. Discs came fast. The job required total concentration. My mind, eyes, and hands focused intensely on the piece of metal. Nothing else existed. But off and on, I did manage to gaze quickly for any suspicious looks as the foreman moved silently among us. Only a few of the assembly workers were foreigners, the majority being Germans—most of them middle-aged or older men (no young ones to be seen) and many women.

A loud whistle announced the beginning and end of the workday. We had time off for lunch and probably coffee breaks, but I don't remember for sure. Everything was new and scary. We worked from 6:00 A.M. until 6:00 P.M., Monday through Friday and until noon on Saturday. Everyone's favorite time was the end of the day. At the first sound of the shrill whistle, all machines stopped, and the noise died abruptly. Tools were cleaned and locked up.

Most German factory workers either avoided us or remained distant. Since few foreigners spoke German, a natural barrier existed. Somehow, a few men noticed that I knew German. Because of my four years of German in the gymnasium back home, I was able to read, write, and speak the language. My vocabulary was limited but grammatically correct.

After a few weeks they transferred us to new jobs. Because of my knowledge of German, I was given an office job; Helka did spray painting. I didn't like her new job. I told her, "Helka, the mask, rubber gloves, and extra food are suspicious. It must be bad for your health."

"Yes, I know," she said. "I'll be careful. I'll be okay." She shared her extra food with me.

This was our first separation. From the time we had left the ghetto, Helka and I had been together day and night. We had become a team, an efficient team, not at all the way it had been at home before the war. My little sister, almost two years younger than me, had been a pest. She wanted the toys I had, the games I played, and she even tried to intrude on my friends. Her nagging and Mother's intervention only made things worse. She was always in my way. Later on, Father liked her help in the coal yard, and everyone thought she was cute. I didn't think I was getting the respect I had coming.

The war changed everything. In the somber mood of the ghetto, we stopped the childish rivalries and went separate ways, she with her friends, I with mine. But, far away from home, in a hostile country, we had become inseparable. We needed each other. We depended on each other. We learned, together, to live with danger. My sister and I looked and listened all the time. We communicated by quick glances. Words came later when we were alone. Quick decisions and sudden changes often followed. We were a solid team, and she a good partner. Helka was practical, decisive and brave.

I liked the office work right away because it kept me away from the dust, noise, and the assembly line. I don't recall the details of the job, but I was able to manage.

One co-worker remains clear in my mind. About seventeen years old [I was nineteen at the time but somehow thought of myself as much older], of small build but with an aggressive manner, he was a proud member of *Hitler Jugend*—Hitler Youth.

One afternoon he and I were developing an x-ray film in a small lab when he began his tirade. "*Unser Führer* [our leader, meaning Hitler] is the savior of the world. His philosophy and plans are magnificent. He is quickly restoring Germany's power. Most of Europe and part of Russia is already ours."

When I brought up neutral Switzerland, he laughed "Neutrality! That's a joke! It will last as long as it's good for us. Then we'll march in. England and America will be next. No one can stop us anymore."

He was anxiously awaiting his eighteenth birthday so he could enlist and be an active participant in conquering the whole world. I realized the danger. If he should ever find out who I really was . . .

15

Slowly I was getting used to living and working among the Germans. The Germans back home in gray uniforms were soldiers with rifles, and the ones in the black uniforms, SS and Gestapo with vicious dogs and leather whips. I knew of their atrocities. I feared them. I hated them. But the Germans here in Neustadt were workers, shopkeepers, fathers, mothers, and children. They were civilians, ordinary people. I witnessed important events in their lives.

A young couple at the train station stood out. The young man was a handsome officer and his wife an elegant, attractive woman. He most likely was being sent east—the dreaded Russian front. First the two of them walked on the platform holding hands and talking quietly. When the train arrived, they were saying good-bye. I could tell they were trying to act dignified, but their fear was obvious. She continued to wave her white handkerchief long after he disappeared in the morning fog.

Another episode took place in the factory. As I entered the large hall during the lunch break, I noticed a cluster of German women at the other end. When I moved closer, I saw a middle-aged woman surrounded by coworkers. Sobbing and unable to speak, she passed around a letter. Her youngest son, an infantry soldier had been badly wounded and neared death. Her friends tried to console the woman but her pain would not ease. My heart went out to her. She had hopes and fears as all people did. I felt torn. She was German and belonged to the very people who had tortured us. They had made a cold, calculated decision to totally destroy all Jews. And they were carrying it out with precision and cruelty. Still, I felt sorry for her.

Ashamed of myself, I still couldn't hate the young couple at the train station or this suffering mother. They were human beings to me.

*   *   *

To add to my confusion came acts of kindness at work. A group of four or five middle-aged men tried to be helpful to my sister and me. They often shared their lunch with us. They asked about our families and life before the occupation. They made predictions of a quick end to the war. These men were not Hitler's followers; they certainly didn't condone his actions. I was surprised that they didn't hide their political opposition.

A soft-spoken man who had the respect of the rest of the group showed the most interest. I had a strange feeling that he suspected that Helka and I were Jewish. Maybe he himself had been a political prisoner in one of the early concentration camps Hitler built for his opponents. He noticed my shoes, the ones that the shoemaker back home had mended many times. Now they were beyond repair. The soles had worn paper thin, had big holes, and the seams had started to come apart. One day, the man's wife brought better shoes for both of us. They weren't new—other women had worn them—and the brown shoes were slightly too large but sturdy and all leather. I liked them a lot. My feet didn't get wet in the rain and snow.

The same man and his wife invited us to his home for Sunday dinner. The small apartment was clean and pleasant—no Hitler pictures on the walls. We ate in the dining room on a table with a white tablecloth. The dishes sparkled. His wife served *Kopfsalat* (young head lettuce salad), tender and succulent *Schweinebraten* (pork roast), *Kartoffel Kloese* (large, fluffy potato dumplings), *Gewurze* (fresh vegetables), dark crusty bread, and, of course, beer. Lots of beer. I had a hard time reconciling that during the raging war against Jews, Helka and I were having Sunday dinner with a German family at their home. I wondered what Father and Natek had for dinner in Piotrkow.

The couple's two teenage children, a boy and a girl, also ate at the table. While the parents carried on a friendly conversation with us, the two of them ate silently. Clearly they did not want us in their home. They ate and left. We definitely saw the political conflict in this family.

* * *

We even experienced acts of kindness from strangers. As Helka and I once wandered through the city, we noticed a small bakery on a quiet side street. The aroma spread for several blocks. People crowded inside. We waited until closing time. When the last customer left, we cautiously entered, and I asked if there was anything left. All baked goods at that time were rationed. The tall, serious-looking owner understood that we are foreigners and had no coupons. Bread and rolls had been sold, but some *Lebkuchen*—ginger bread cookies—were left. He sold them to us, though doing so was illegal. The cookies, rectangular and of good size, had a whitish, shiny surface. As I bit into one, a sweet, ginger flavor filled my mouth. It tasted heavenly. We became steady customers. I still love those cookies.

* * *

Another episode still comes fresh to my mind. On a cold winter day, Helka and I were returning to the *Lager* (the camp) after a long day at the factory. We were walking down the street when I felt an urge to urinate. The bladder infection I had developed in the ghetto was getting worse. A stream of warm urine coursed down my legs, soaking my long stockings. We went into the small courtyard of an apartment building. I looked around to make sure that no one saw us and began to remove the cold, wet stockings. I had almost finished when a second floor window opened, and a gray-haired woman said something I couldn't quite hear. Suddenly, stockings floated down. One pair, after another. Thick, soft, warm cotton stockings. She smiled, shut the window and vanished.

* * *

Meanwhile, we began to adjust to life in the *Lager* and its strict routine. At 5:00 A.M., Herr Uhlman came in, turned on the lights (it was early winter so it was still dark outside) and blew his whistle. The large hall came alive instantly.

We all jumped out of bed, put on our clothes and washed quickly at one of the sinks lined up against the wall. We showered in another building, used mostly evenings and on Sundays. For breakfast, we had dark bread, margarine, and watery coffee. Within a short time, everyone left, rushing in different directions for their work assignments.

The end of the day was more relaxed. We all arrived from various jobs, hungry and ready to eat. Supper consisted mostly of rutabaga soup (some days less watery than others), potatoes or cabbage, and bread. Meat, mostly pork roast, was rare, appearing on holidays and Sundays. We all hoped for seconds and thicker soup from the bottom of the large pot. Bread had become a delicacy. Hunger never quite went away.

After lingering awhile in the dining hall, everyone headed for the bunk beds. Each bed had a straw mattress, a flat pillow, and two gray blankets. We kept our possessions either at the foot of the bed or underneath it. The bunk beds became our mini-homes. Not only did we sleep there, but we also read letters, mended our clothes and visited with other women. The latest news about the war spread around, as well as gossip, and most important, stories about life back home. Many friendships developed. Helka and I mingled freely, participated in conversations but avoided closer contacts. We felt safer that way. Like many of the other women, before we went to sleep, Helka and I knelt on the beds, crossed ourselves, kissed the small medallions on our neck chains and prayed. This became our nightly, visible routine.

At 10:00 P.M. sharp, Herr Uhlman came again. He walked through the aisles, checked for anyone missing, turned off the lights and locked the door. The darkness did not stop the conversations right away. It took awhile for the voices to die down.

*　*　*

The initially blurry picture of the women in the *Lager* began to resolve. The group was not homogenous. I detected several small groups with distinct differences—Ukrainians and Russians who behaved well and kept to themselves; Polish women, young peasant girls, mostly timid and homesick along with six or seven tough ones. These were loud, aggressive and vulgar. They used foul language, wore loud clothes and excessive makeup. They bragged about sex with the POWs of various nationalities. They stayed out late, broke curfew and missed work. These few women intimidated all of us, but not Herr Uhlman. Herr Uhlman, the one in charge of the *Lager* of several hundred women, was a middle-aged, sturdy man with a mild manner. He seemed fair and easy, but he could be strict and severe. He knew how to handle rough women, and they feared him. I didn't like those women either, but as long as they didn't suspect us, I didn't care. And for a while no one did.

16

Our lives in Neustadt fell into a comfortable routine. We each had a job, shelter, and food. We had left behind the fear of not making it from one day to the next in the dangerous Polish part of our hometown. Work at the factory seemed to be going well, the *Lager* and bunk beds—our own bunk beds—felt almost luxurious, and the three meals a day, no matter how skimpy, seemed a wonder after the ghetto and life on the run. It felt great. In our free time, we began to explore the city.

Neustadt/Orla was a clean and orderly small town. The houses looked well kept up, sidewalks free of snow and roads easily passable. We saw no bomb ruins. The city remained intact. It must have been beautiful in the summer, when the Orla River flowed and the parks filled with people. The center of town had a vibrant life. People filled the streets in the mornings and late afternoons, but quieted from 1:00 to 3:00 P.M. during *Mahlzeit* (mealtime). All stores and offices shut down. Not our factory, however. Everyone knew the rule and obeyed it. Mothers with small children, bundled in warm clothes, rushed into the stores before closing time. Occasionally, a frustrated customer pulled and knocked in vain on a locked door. He or she walked away empty-handed even though the storeowner moved around inside.

The food supplies though not generous remained adequate. Maybe meat was scarce, but bread, rolls, fruits, and vegetables always seemed to be available. Customers had to bring their ration cards and their own papers bags, which they used many times. Most people walked on foot or rode bicycles in warmer weather. Few people owned private cars; everyone relied on street-cars.

Saturday was the day of frenzied preparation for Sunday. Women shopped, cooked and baked. Men relaxed in the *Bierstube* (bars) with huge mugs of beer, and noisy children played in the snow. Sunday was the day of rest. A mood of peace rested on the air. Church bells rang, and families dressed in their finest walked briskly to hear their Lutheran ministers. In good weather, people took walks along the tree-lined streets, greeted their friends and neighbors, and exchanged the latest news. In the winter of 1942-1943, all of Europe suffered, but life was good in Neustadt/Orla.

On one of those pleasant Sundays, as Helka and I walked near a park, I suddenly startled. A young man across the street, who had just turned a corner, looked like Richard, the young man from the ghetto. His profile and even his gait was absolutely his. My heart skipped a beat.

I crossed the street and followed him. After a few steps . . . a let down. It wasn't Richard, it couldn't have been. It was my wishful thinking.

*   *   *

Meanwhile, in the *Lager*, I was becoming aware of a small group of women, the so-called "city girls." Because there were few of them, they stood out more. I still remember some of them. An older woman, she must have been in her middle or late thirties, was small, slender, wore stylish clothes and had good manners. Her eyes fascinated me—one brown, the other one green-ish. She had a younger friend, and the two of them kept to themselves. I also spotted two young women with expensive, elegant clothes. Halina, a blue-eyed blonde, and Zosia (Sophia), with a darker complexion. They were tall and striking. Halina seemed gentle and dignified. She tried to mix with others but inspired awe and respect, and everyone kept at a distance. Zosia, also beautiful, with her dark curly hair and lively eyes, was outgoing, accessible, and mingled with everyone. Halina and Zosia both came from Warsaw; they spent a lot of time together and could have been friends from way back.

The country girls, who were the majority, and the city girls, mixed unpredictably. The confident ones let their curiosity lead them and mixed easily with the city girls. They frequently borrowed their clothes for dates. The shy ones seemed overwhelmed, uncomfortable, and stayed away. There was nothing unusual about Helka and me. We were not striking, our clothes inexpensive. Still, we were considered city girls.

As I began to pay attention, I noticed more about the city girls and began to worry. There were Jews among the city girls. I could tell, but luckily the Polish women could not.

Christmas was approaching; anticipation and excitement filled in the air. Many women wrote letters and sent small gifts to their families and friends. The usually scarce mail from home grew considerably. Everyone waited anxiously to hear Herr Uhlman call her name. Letters and packages brought tears of joy and tears of loneliness.

The two of us watched and worried. Nobody wrote to us. Then one day, a letter came from our friends Danka and Mala back home. It included a short, cautious letter from Father with good news: he and Natek, still in Piotrkow, worked in the same Forced Labor Camp. In spite of repeated deportations, the two of them remained together. I wrote back about our factory and the German coworkers. I described the *Lager*, the food we ate, and the women with whom we lived. In the midst of the raging war against the Jews, our correspondence seemed like a miracle. Two Jews in Poland communicating in the open with two Jews in Germany. And *Die Deutsche Post* (the German Postal Service) carried these communications with their renown precision. We knew the risks, especially for our friends. Every letter we received, we read several times and then destroyed.

A letter from "home" always became a happy event for us. Except one. It came late in the spring of 1943. In addition to the usual news, Danka wrote with great admiration about the Warsaw Ghetto Uprising. "The brave Jewish fighters inflicted heavy losses on the Germans." I was petrified. Why should a Polish girl in Piotrkow, Poland, write to another Polish girl in Neustadt, Germany, about the Jews? I tore up that letter right away. Our correspondence lasted close to two years, and none of the letters were censored.

*   *   *

At last, we had the Christmas party. The food was better and plentiful. We had a holiday meal with the usual pork roast, potato dumplings, plenty of crusty bread, and pudding. Some women shared their cookies from home. The Christmas tree gleamed with brightly lit candles. We listened to the harmonica and sang Christmas carols. We admired each other's clothes and hair styles, even though very little had changed or looked new. The two of us participated enthusiastically in the festivities. One of the women approached me with a Christmas wafer. I said a prayer, crossed myself, broke off a piece, and put it in my mouth. As she moved on to the next person, Halinka came around from the back and whispered, "The piece you broke off was too large. It should have been quite small."

She gave me a smile and disappeared. I quickly looked around, but everyone looked busy and happy.

Before long, winter's end was in sight. The days grew longer, and the snow melted quickly. Instead of the blustery cold wind, we felt a soft, warm breeze. Spring was on its way. I continued to watch each new transport arriving at the *Lager*. I saw Jews among the new women. No one seemed to notice them, and they adjusted quickly.

* * *

Helka and I had adjusted well to our situation and work. For us, all went well until the arrival of two sisters. The two girls—I was sure they were sisters—had good Aryan looks and spoke accent-free Polish. Their clothes looked simple and modest. They could easily have passed as Poles if it wasn't for their fear. That was a give-away. It was palpable. They were timid, moved cautiously and stayed out of everyone's way. Their eyes had a sad and frightened cast. I knew they must have just escaped some unspeakable horror.

The Polish women spotted them right away. They began to whisper. The *Lager* became dangerous. Helka and I had to talk about this new situation. We took a long walk away from the *Lager*. I felt we had to leave and soon. Helka opposed that plan. "Where will we go, and what will we do? We have a roof over our heads, food, work, and you want to leave it all? The excitement will pass. We will be okay."

I knew better. "The whispers will become louder. Soon they will talk openly. They'll start to look around for other Jews. Someone eventually will report us. Then it will be too late."

Finally, Helka agreed.

17

We took long walks to make our plans, trying to decide what day would be best, how to leave the Lager without being too noticeable, and where we should go when we got away. We had not even left, and the whole thing seemed scary already. Staying or leaving began to look equally dangerous. Still we made our plans.

As I studied the map, I noticed that going straight south from Neustadt led us to Switzerland. Once there, we should be able to cross the border. I could see the two of us out of Germany, out of danger. That was a long way off. Our first challenge—to pack our suitcases without being noticed. This proved to be difficult in an open hallway. We informed the women next to us that our winter clothes needed airing—a substitute to dry cleaning and a well-known method back home. We took our coats and dresses outside, shook them a few times, but, instead of bringing them back inside, we put them quickly into the suitcases. Then we hid the small suitcases between the bushes in the backyard.

We decided to escape on Friday evening. Since work on Saturday ended at noon, many women skipped it and got by. The foreman never called Herr Uhlman before Monday. By then, we should be safely far away.

On Friday evening, we casually joined a group of women going into town. When we got outside the building, we let the women go on ahead while we pretended to wait for someone. Our suitcases remained hidden in the same place. We picked them up, walked away briskly from the *Lager* and headed towards the railroad station. No trains left for a while, and, since we didn't feel safe waiting in the lobby, we continued to walk the dark streets.

When we returned, the small lobby had been lit and had filled with people. Soldiers stood with their wives or girlfriends, families with children waited in groups, and single travelers milled about. While the civilians were loud and lively, the soldiers looked subdued and somber. We blended in easily with the crowd. Already a good-size group crowded in front of the door leading to the platform. It should open any minute. I stood in line for the tickets, quite close to the window, when a loud: *"Achtung, Achtung!"* ("Attention, Attention!") could be heard.

Several armed policemen forced their way in. They locked the front door and demanded everyone's *Kennkarte* (ID). Cards appeared quickly. The soldiers had progressed halfway through the crowd when a loud voice shouted: *"Hier sind die Franzosische Schweine!"* ("The French pigs are here!")

The soldiers pushed three young men outside. Helka and I exchanged quick looks and headed towards the back door. Too late. A stocky, middle-aged policeman stood in front of us. As we handed him our papers, he called to his partners, *"Ich habe zwei Polinen!"* ("I have two Polish women!") "Arrest them!" came the reply.

They shoved us towards the French POWs, whose escape plan apparently had been foiled by an informer. The ride in the police van seemed very long. It was late when we arrived at the small police station. The place was poorly lit and silent. They put Helka and me in a cell close to the entrance and the French men way down the hall. The grumpy guard shut the heavy door with a loud bang, and locked it with several keys.

The echo of the shuffling feet and clanking keys bounced off the high ceiling of the hallway. After the sounds died down, the stillness overwhelmed us. Our cell felt and smelled like a cave. After my eyes adjusted to the blackness, I could make out the shapes of the two narrow cots against the opposite walls, a toilet, and a small window with iron cross bars. The window was way up high and faced more darkness. I suddenly realized that we were in prison, in a German prison. The events of the day raced through my mind. We could have done nothing differently to avoid this capture. We knew we had to get ready for the interrogation. It could come anytime. In hushed voices, we repeated the story of one mother and two fathers, to explain our different last names. "Do you think they'll believe us? We were born twenty-two months apart—not much time to lose a husband, find another one and have a second child." whispered Helka.

"I know, I know, but we better memorize all the names."

We decided that Helka, who understood German because of her knowledge of Yiddish, would smile, nod, and repeat "*Nix verstehen*"—"nothing to understand." I would be the translator and speaker. Finally exhaustion forced us to rest. We lay down on one of the cots—we didn't want to be apart —and tried to sleep. My sleep was shallow and splintered. Each time I woke, a cold wave of panic wrapped around me.

I was wide awake when he came for us. The same silent guard unlocked the heavy door and motioned us to follow him. The walk wasn't far. We entered a spacious, bright office. Hitler's picture faced us. No one waited for us. The large desk had stacks of papers, a family photo of a young woman with windblown short hair and two little boys clinging to her skirt, and a telephone.

Suddenly the door opened and a man entered. Of large frame, with full, reddish face and a receding hairline, he didn't wear a black uniform—he was not Gestapo. Our false papers lay in front of him. He studied them carefully, looking at the pictures and each of us. He asked for the name of our workplace and the *Lager* in which we lived. Then came the question: "What were you doing last night, after the curfew, at the railroad station?"

I had a ready answer. I cleared my throat, steadied my voice and replied: "Ever since we have arrived in Neustadt/Orla, Mother has written to us at least once a week. Now it's been more than a month since her last letter. We were worried. We planned to visit her and come back."

He seemed surprised at my German.

I tried to read his face. It was blank. He began to dial the phone. I felt sure he was calling the Gestapo. I listened in: "*Guten Morgan, Herr Uhlman. Es ist der Kommandant der Polizei.*" "This is the Police Commander. I have two Polish women from your *Lager*. Can you come over?"

What a relief. Herr Uhlman seemed a great improvement over the Gestapo, but I wondered what he would say. We had broken the curfew and tried to escape, and they had caught us at the station. The police officer busied himself with other papers as we waited.

Shortly, Herr Uhlman appeared at the door. He was not surprised to see us. He pulled up a chair and listened as the Kommandant repeated my story. "They wanted to visit their mother in Poland . . . and they planned to come back." He gave us a skeptical look. "What do you know about them?"

Herr Uhlman glanced at us again. "The two girls are hard workers, they are liked at the factory and well-behaved in my *Lager*. They obviously don't understand our German laws. They should have talked to me first. Please let them go. The foreman needs them at work. It's hard to find replacements."

The Kommandant was surprised, but he agreed.

* * *

It was still Saturday morning when we returned to the *Lager*. Herr Uhlman went back to his office. In all outward ways, the ordeal had ended. I had had a feeling all along that Herr Uhlman like the two of us, but what he had done for us that day—unbelievable. Without his help, the police officer would have investigated us and easily discovered that no one with our names existed. The documents, as we well knew, were forged. It would have been the end for us. Herr Uhlman must have suspected that we were Jewish and decided to save us.

Still, the events of the last few hours refused to leave my mind. We sat in the quiet hall, trying to come to grips with the ordeal. The *Lager* was quiet as most everybody had gone to work. A few night-shift women remained but slept soundly. We began to unpack our small suitcases, when Zosia, the striking, dark haired woman—only a few years older than I—waved at me from a quiet corner. "You can't stay here," she whispered when I joined her. "Last night a few women noticed that you were missing, and I heard them shout: the two sisters who ran away are Jews. They belong in the ghetto. Let's send them back. You have to go. The women will be back from work soon. Walk to the next town and don't carry the suitcases. I would go myself if I weren't so easy to spot. The two of you blend in much better."

I suddenly realized that Zosia also wanted to escape. She was Jewish. Helka and I had no choice; we had to run again. The extra clothes we put on were somewhat uncomfortable but didn't show. We hid the suitcases under the bunk beds, looked around the large hall and left quickly. I didn't dare look back, and I was sure someone would come after us. It was a relief to reach the center of town, which bustled with the usual Saturday activities.

We had to decide again where to go. Large signs on the roads listed names and distances of the nearby towns. I don't remember the name of the town we picked, but it took us several hours to get there. The sun gave way to clouds while we walked on the open roads. Since we wore all the clothes we possessed, the rain could have been a disaster. We couldn't have gone to the train station soaking wet, and there was no place to hide. Luckily, it didn't rain.

The city we reached was larger than Neustadt, and the station busier then the one in which we were arrested the night before. I did not want to think about that. A large map covered part of one wall. Next to it hung a schedule of train departures and arrivals from various cities. We had to pick our first destination. I chose Nürnberg. Many people traveled to this large city. Nürnberg lay quite a bit south of Neustadt in the state of Bavaria, and Bavaria was located closer to Switzerland. It should be easy to reach the border from there.

* * *

Buying the tickets came next. Only one of us should walk up to the ticket window. Why endanger both? I would be the one because of my knowledge of German. The lines were long but moved steadily. As I slowly advanced, I rehearsed the few words I had to say, worked on my smile and composure. I didn't want to call any attention to myself. I could pass as a young German woman. I would. As I moved closer to the window, the man in front of me took a long time. He had many questions. The blond woman in the dark uniform behind the window was getting irritated. Finally she handed him the ticket, looked at the long line, and impatiently said: "*Nachst?*" ("Next?") I moved up. I skipped the smile. With a steady voice and in my best German, I asked for two tickets to Nürnberg. She took the money I put down, tore two tickets off a large spool, and caounted out my change. She glanced at me, pushed the tickets and the *Deutsche Marks* and *Phennigs* (German Marks and pennies) through the window. Across the lobby, Helka's eyes never left me even once.

* * *

We had a half hour wait until departure. We did not wait at the station but walked in the busy streets. When we returned, a loudspeaker announced the arrival of our train. Boarding began. We walked out on the platform and quickly split up. Helka boarded the train through the back door and I through the front. We planned to travel in the same car but sit far apart. If one of us got caught, it wouldn't endanger the other one.

* * *

Since I bought the cheapest tickets, we had no private compartments or individual seats. Rows of hard wooden benches, with four to five seats each stretched from front to back. Passengers streamed in. There was no pushing or shoving. Only *Bitte schön, danke schön* (Please and thank you) could be heard. Since the aisle seat was already occupied, I had to take the second seat in the middle row. I glanced to the back and saw my sister in an aisle seat. That seat was an important strategic spot. If we would see that the conductor, who checked the tickets, also asked for the *Kennkarte* (ID), it would mean trouble. We would have to leave right away. The rest room or the adjoining car would be the place to hide, and the aisle seats gave us quickest exit.

After the suitcases had been put away and everyone seated, the heavy doors shut with a loud bang. Outside on the platform, the conductor waved a small flag, shouted something I couldn't hear and blew his whistle. A sudden jerk shook the car. The wheels began to move with a screeching noise. The slow pace became faster and faster and gave way to a rhythmic shaking. Patches of dirty snow on the bare ground and tall, naked trees quickly slid past the windows. This was in the cold, early spring of 1943.

* * *

The passengers—the usual mixture of soldiers, civilians, and families—started to get comfortable. Mothers reached for food for their children, some men and women read, and others settled for a nap. On my right, a husky man wearing a felt hat with a feather watched the landscape through the window. On my left, an older lady with neatly combed gray hair and an impeccable white blouse began to crochet what seemed to be a large mitten. She gave me a friendly look, and I could tell she was ready to start a conversation—something too dangerous for me. I didn't return her look, slid down on the bench, turned the other way and pretended to sleep.

I was far from sleeping. Thoughts of the last twenty-four hours raced through my mind. We had made it into the train, but we weren't safe yet. Now we had to pass as Germans. If the conductor, who would arrive any minute, should ask for our *Kennkarte*, the Polish false papers would not protect us. Only Germans could travel on trains. Poles were not allowed to leave their workplaces. He would surely ask: "Where do you work, and why aren't you there?"

I would have no answer. My head began to spin. Through my half-closed eyes, I began to watch everyone around me. Nothing had changed. The passengers read, talked, slept. The husky man next to the window still seemed absorbed in the monotonous landscape. The older lady continued to crochet with the same enthusiasm; only her blouse began to show a few wrinkles. No one paid any attention to me. The continuous clack, clack, clack of the wheels became soothing. I must have dozed off.

A gentle nudge woke me up. The lady next to me kept repeating, *"Fraulein, Fraulein,"* and pointed toward the aisle. An older, tall man in a conductor's uniform waited. *"Fahrkarte"* ("Ticket"), he said and looked at me with an unsmiling face. I hoped he could not see my hand tremble as I reached for my muff, unzipped the small compartment, took out the ticket and gave it to him. He examined the ticket and asked *"Nürnberg?"*

"Jawohl" ("Yes"), I answered and waited. From the black leather bag hanging over his left shoulder, he took out a small metal punch, made a hole in the middle of the ticket and passed it back to me. He didn't ask for the *Kennkarte.*

An eternity passed before he checked my sister's ticket and left the car through the back door.

*   *   *

The sun rose as we arrived in Nürnberg. The city still slept. Street sweepers and stray dogs had the streets all to themselves. The large, impressive city had a medieval flavor. The tall, ornate buildings made the cobblestone streets narrow and dim. Durer's artwork appeared everywhere. I don't remember any ruins. After a short walk, we returned to the train station.

Only one more part of our trip remained. From the map on the wall of the station lobby we picked a town close to the Swiss border. We could easily be there by the next day and leave Germany forever. Luckily, I checked the price of the ticket before going to the window.

The small town next to Switzerland was out of our reach. We didn't have enough money. What we had earned in Neustadt in the past few months, even though we saved everything, was not enough. I had no sense of the value of the money, because we couldn't use it. Since the *Lager* provided the food and lodging, we received no coupons, a must for any purchase.

I had overestimated the few hundred *Deutsche Marks* when making our escape plans. The furthest city south we could reach was Regensburg. Regensburg, nowhere near Switzerland, lay in the middle of Bavaria, south of Nürnberg and north of Munich.

18

We reached Regensburg—a city much larger than Neustadt/Orla with wider streets, grass, and trees—early in the morning. Men and women, all in a hurry, filled the sidewalks and clamoring streetcars. The town awoke already busy. We would have loved to walk and observe the city, but it was time to face reality. We had to find the *Arbeitsamt* (the employment office), and face the German officials, in order to get a job.

We asked directions and were sent to a large, impressive building close to the center of town. As we entered a room on the main floor, a civilian man sat at a large desk facing a window and a young woman sat at a smaller one closer to the door. The man in his late forties was of light complexion and pleasant manner. He turned towards us with a friendly look. He made me feel at ease. After a short greeting, I began the well-rehearsed story:

"The two of us are sisters, stepsisters actually (different last names), from Poland. Back home we volunteered for work in Germany. We were already on a train with a large group of Polish men and women headed for our destination somewhere in Bavaria. We did not know the name of the city. In Breslau we had a layover for several hours. Instead of waiting at the railroad station, we decided, as did some others in our group, to see the city." That part of the story was true; our original transport did stop in Breslau, close to the Polish border, and we did spend some time in the city. "We were not gone very long, but when we returned, the train wasn't there. It had left with the rest of the group and our suitcases. We tried in vain to catch up with them. I was hoping that you would be able to help us find our group."

I hoped that after hearing my story he would say: "Oh, well, the two of you had volunteered for work in Germany when you lost your transport. It will be easier to find work for you here than to search all over." But he didn't. In fact, he didn't say anything. He listened, scribbled something on a piece of paper and made no comment. He asked for our documents, checked them carefully and, pointing to the young woman, said, "*Die Fraulein* . . . will take you across the street to another office to find your transport," and he handed her our papers.

* * *

The office building across the street, also a large brick building similar to the employment office, was somewhat taller and set back into a more isolated area. As we got closer to the entrance, I noticed a red flag with a black swastika in the center. The Nazi flag. We faced the Gestapo building. The long hallways had pictures of Hitler, Goebbels, and Goering.

The young woman took us to an office on the second floor. A map of occupied Europe left little space on a large wall. Red lines with black dots ran from country to country. A short, wiry, uniformed man entered a few minutes later. I noticed he had darting, suspicious eyes. The *fraulein* told him that her boss needed his help. She repeated our story, put the false papers in front of him and left. He studied our documents, looked at us and said: "So, you volunteered for work in Germany?"

"*Jawohl,*" I answered.

"You left the train in Breslau for a short time and missed it?"

"Yes," I nodded.

"And the two of you, straight from Poland, all on your own, traveled halfway across Germany looking for your transport?"

I did not like the tone of his voice, but I nodded again. Before I knew it, he stood in front of me, shouting: "Stop lying!"

His hand landed on my face. It was a hard slap. My head shook violently, and a burning spread over my cheek. He was furious and continued to shout. "Where are you coming from, and you better tell the truth."

I thought I saw his hand raise again.

Suddenly two men in the black Gestapo uniforms appeared at the door. They raised their right arms in salute, said *"Heil Hitler, Herr Lieutenant, we are ready."*

He looked at us with terrifying coldness in his eyes, told us to stay there and left. We didn't dare move.

The next half-hour or forty-five minutes seemed to last forever. My left cheek burned, my back ached, and my legs were getting stiff. Thoughts of Auschwitz raced through my mind.

The officer seemed distracted when he returned. He picked up the phone and asked for someone. A stocky woman came in. "Do a body search on them," he said.

We followed her to the basement. In a dimly lit room with a large table and a couple of chairs, she told us to undress, undress completely. As we stood naked, she spread our clothes on the table and turned the coats, dresses and underwear inside out. She even tried to lift the lining of our shoes. Suspicious, she proceeded slowly. Finally, she picked up my muff. This was my first muff. When the tailor back home made my winter coat, I had begged my mother for a matching muff. Most of my friends already had them. After a short resistance, she had agreed.

The beautiful muff—both stylish and practical—was my hand warmer and a purse. I used it all winter. The woman took her time with it. First she unzipped the small compartment, removed every item and examined them closely. Then she put her hand inside and felt around. I wasn't worried. I knew the contents well. I had checked them several times before we escaped from the *Lager*. Suddenly, she pulled out a small, white piece of paper. What it was and its source, I had no idea. She began to unfold it before I recognized it—a coupon for a bar of soap. Helka had gotten it in the factory because of her paint-spraying job. The coupon had the name and address of the factory.

I felt my face getting fire red. Luckily she was busy unfolding the coupon and didn't look at me. I had only seconds to gain my composure when she asked: "You are coming straight from Poland and have a German coupon for soap?"

"Oh, we got that in Breslau. A Polish woman we met gave it to us when we ran out of soap. I don't quite know how to use it."

She seemed to vacillate as she looked at the two of us. Slowly, she folded the coupon, put it in her own pocket and told us to get dressed. I slid my hands into the muff as soon as she gave it back to me. The softness and warmth felt good, but one of my fingers got stuck. I felt carefully. I discovered a tear, a tiny tear in the lining. That's where the small piece of paper had been, and in spite of several checks, I had missed it.

I somehow got permission to go to the bathroom. I flushed down a partly used bar of our own soap, which I found in the small carry-on bag, which somehow had been overlooked.

*　*　*

When we returned to the office upstairs, civilian and uniformed Gestapo rushed in and out, their voices loud and agitated. The phone rang constantly. Something major had happened. Our lieutenant had left. A civilian man took us in tow. He kept the soap coupon, gave us our papers and sent us back to the employment office.

The employment official looked stunned to see us. He said, "You're back? They let you go? What about your transport?" He looked at us in disbelief. "My, my, they didn't arrest them," he muttered to himself. "So, you can stay in Regensburg, and they want me to find you jobs?" He scratched his head. "That shouldn't be too hard. Let me see," and he opened a large notebook.

"Please, could we work on a farm?" I asked. A remote farm in the country would be safe.

"The two of you on a farm?" He burst out laughing. "The farmers would hate me. You're not country girls." He shook his head and continued to turn the pages. "I have families that need housekeepers," he said.

"Could we work in the same place?" I interrupted. "We would like, if possible, to stay together."

"No, only one person per family," he said firmly. In the short silence that followed, I saw the two of us in a new *Lager* facing the same danger. He finished scanning the pages, closed the notebook and asked the secretary for another one. This notebook was thicker and his progress through it slow.

"I do have a hospital looking for help, but not foreigners," and he kept going. Suddenly he stopped on one page, focused on something, looked at us and said with a smile, "I have it. A hotel. The Maximilian Hotel could use both of you."

We exchanged a quick look and Helka joined me in "*Danke schön, danke schön.*"

19

As we approached the Maximilian Hotel, I found it overwhelming. The hotel, in the center of the picturesque old town, occupied a whole block close to the railroad station and a park—a most desirable location. The smooth limestone walls and intricate baroque sculpting on the tall doors and windows gave the edifice an old, majestic appearance. The hotel, where we would work and live, looked like a palace compared to the barracks we had left. For how long? Our fear returned. The man at the Gestapo office had kept the soap coupon with the address of the factory in Neustadt. After they finished their major case, the Gestapo might get back to our matter. If they checked, they would learn we had run away from there and quickly find out why. The consequences of that . . . I couldn't think of a way out. Instead, I focused on the hotel.

The hotel's interior matched its elegant exterior. After a short interview, Frau Wittner, the owner, glanced at our false papers, asked about previous work experience and called Ursula, her niece and assistant, a tall young woman who treated Frau Wittner more like a boss than her aunt. Frau Wittner told her to take us to our room and have us start work the next day at 6:00 A.M. As we followed Ursula's brisk, long strides, we listened to the clatter of the handful of keys at her belt. She said we could have dinner that night and took us to our room.

The room, on the fourth, the top, floor of the hotel, had a low ceiling next to the large window, making it look like an attic. Spacious and full of light, it had a beautiful view of a park. Only one person shared it with us, and she was at work. For a little while it was all ours. As we sat down, we exchanged glances of disbelief. No more huge, open hall packed with bunk beds and women around whom we had to be so careful. These beds had sturdy wooden frames, firm mattresses with no straw, lots of bedding, and colorful spreads on top. I couldn't resist. We sank into them with our heads deep in the clean, soft pillows. What was meant to be a short nap became a deep, dreamless sleep. It was morning when Elsa, our roommate, awakened us.

The employee eating area was located in the basement next to the main kitchen. Women ate in a hurry, exchanged a few words and left. We followed Elsa, and the cook dished out hot, thick oatmeal with milk and sugar, a large slice of bread with margarine, and coffee with sugar and milk. The portions were generous and seconds available. When Helka and I started the breakfast, we watched each other not to eat too fast or too much.

The Maximilian Hotel in Regensburg, Germany, a town with a 2,000-year history.

* * *

Ursula waited for us in her office, and she had our jobs ready. My sister became a dishwasher and I a cleaning girl. We started right away. Helka worked on the main floor across from the dining room in a small room with a sink and a long row of cabinets. She washed only the glasses, cups, and saucers that were not returned to the kitchen in the basement like the rest of the dishes. They were kept handy because the waiters needed them all the time and had little patience. Especially Herr Bauer, the head waiter. An older man with a sullen face and a stiff, well-trimmed mustache, he wore an impeccable dark suit with a bow tie. A starched white napkin hung over his left arm. The napkin, mostly used to remove crumbs from the linen tablecloths, but sometimes used to express anger as Herr Bauer hit the napkin against anything near him—a table, a counter, even a person. And he mumbled curses. He always found faults with the waiters: their appearance was not professional enough, their service too slow, or they chatted with guests too long. His orders—either angry hisses or shouts. He often tried to catch my sister with her hands out of the sink. At first she would ask: "He is so rude and looks at me in a strange way. Do you think he suspects something?"

"Did he ask any questions?"

"No, not really. It's the looks that scare me."

"Well, maybe you are imagining it. He's the same with the others."

Helka found working with the young waitresses easy, and gradually she became comfortable in her job. She learned to work quickly during the busy hours and slow down later. No one ever had to wait for a cup or saucer. She worked from 6:00 A.M. until 3:00 P.M. and from 5:00 P.M. until 8:00 P.M. When the dining room closed mid-afternoons, she had her break.

* * *

I became one of the *Hausmädchen*—cleaning girls—a crew for heavy work. The *Zimmermädchen*—chambermaids—had the easy job. They made the beds, swept the floors, dusted the furniture and cleaned the bathrooms. Every day they cleaned the same rooms for the same guests. They wore dark dresses with white aprons and small caps. They looked down on us.

Our crew did the heavy work, and we were everywhere. We worked from 6:00 A.M. until 6:00 P.M., Monday through Saturday. With heavy, clumsy equipment, we vacuumed and shampooed the carpets in the hallways. The wooden floors we scrubbed by hand. The job I hated the most—cleaning up after painters or repairmen. They always left messes. We had to move furniture and clean windows splashed with paint. Ursula always looked over our shoulders.

The cleaning crew consisted of Mina, Anne, and myself. Mina, a woman in her thirties, evoked respect. Her blonde hair neatly gathered in a bun and her freshly starched and pressed clothes matched her meticulous work and the attention she paid to detail. Her honesty and fairness made her an exemplary boss. She seemed friendly but reserved; we knew little about her private life.

Anne, the complete opposite, was untidy, her work sloppy, and she nibbled all day long to fill her skinny body. She talked nonstop to anyone who would listen. Because Mina avoided her, I became her confidante. Every morning, she had a lot to tell me, mostly about the dimly lit, smoke filled, *Bierstube* on *Wagner Strasse*—her favorite nightspot. Many other *Frauleins* met young soldiers there. Anne had met Hans. To the rhythm of the loud music, their bodies pressed hard against each other until they disappeared into the darkness of the night.

"Hans is a simple country boy, but he is . . . good," she whispered. "We are meeting again tonight." But, the next morning she talked about Fritz. Hans never showed up.

Anne's desire to have a child was never fulfilled. She announced many pregnancies, but no baby. Co-workers used the old German saying: "The grass that's trampled too much will never grow. Anne's life was a hopeless struggle.

Both women treated me nicely. The three of us did most of the work together, except washing windows. Because Mina and Anne could not tolerate heights, they passed

Helka and I at the Maximilian Hotel. July 1944.

91

the job to me, together with taking off and hanging the heavy brocade drapes. I did all the windows of the dining room, ballroom, lobby, and the hallways. And they were huge and tall. First I climbed to the top of the ladder, placed my two pails, one with hot sudsy water for washing and the other with cold, clear water for rinsing. I washed, rinsed and polished the glass using cloth and leather rags.

When I finished the job, not a smudge or streak could be found on the tall, imposing windows. I was proud of my work. Frau Wittner considered the windows an important part of the hotel's appearance. The hotel had to be worthy of its elite clientele. After checking on me personally, she would walk away without a complaint.

Several weeks elapsed since our escape from Neustadt, and no Gestapo came for us. My fears began to fade. Even though we had ended up in Bavaria, a state in southern Germany nowhere near the Swiss border, I liked it.

Regensburg had a population of close to a hundred thousand people and was one of the larger cities in the state. Its history traced back to pre-Roman times. By the Middle Ages, it had already grown wealthy and powerful; the old part of town still showed this past. Because most Bavarians were Catholic, they had many beautiful old churches. The resonating sounds of the largest two-steeple church reached the whole city. A church clock announced the time every fifteen minutes. The narrow cobblestone streets were clean and full of life. The river Danube, not as blue as in the songs, added a lot of charm. Large and small boats crossed the waters, fishermen pulled up their catch, and many people, especially young couples, took long walks along its shores. A long walk with Richard? It would have been great. Of course.

Few had cars; people walked or rode the screechy streetcar to get around. The citizens, mostly civilians, with only a few soldiers, looked well-dressed, well-nourished and content. As in Neustadt, life in Regensburg seemed good. We saw no signs of war.

* * *

The Maximilian Hotel had two entrances. The elegant park entrance with its wide glass door reaching the ceiling led to a small lobby. The desk of the concierge, a large Persian rug, and shimmering chandeliers dominated the space. The side door off busy Maximilian Street looked less elaborate but was used more frequently. The dining room opened off that entrance. Large windows facing the park took up a whole wall. Light through the airy, delicate drapes flooded the room and created a pleasant, cheerful mood. The white linen tablecloths, porcelain china, and crystal glasses sparkled on the tables. A long, graceful stairway wound its way to the top floor. This gave the hotel a light, open feeling.

The ballroom was magnificent. Huge and rectangular, it had several Persian rugs and tall windows with heavy brocade drapes. Elegant sofas, armchairs and a large Steinway piano had been placed there for comfort and relaxation. This room spoke of luxury, maybe too much luxury for 1943. I found a comparison of life in this hotel and the ghetto back home hard to equate or comprehend.

*　*　*

The few men among the thirty-five to forty hotel employees held the highest positions: the kitchen chef, the headwaiter, and the concierge. Most of them had families and lived in town. The concierge, whose desk faced the main entrance door, was a stocky man, carefully dressed and pompous. A monocle always rested on his nose. As the first one to greet the guests, he showed extreme politeness to the high-ranking military men and rudeness to all others. Something about him scared me. I tried to avoid him.

The women, who ranged in age from their teens to their sixties, were either single or had children with no fathers. They lived in the hotel, and the grandparents took care of their children. They talked about their kids a lot. The single mothers were widely respected, even admired. They helped the *Führer* build the "Great Germany." The hotel women constantly looked for dates. When any of them found a boyfriend, their self-esteem rose, and the others tried not to show their envy. Romances never lasted too long as the soldiers were moved from place to place. The dreaded Eastern Front constantly demanded new supplies of men. Some of the women were brave or desperate enough to date foreigners. They dated foreign workers or prisoners of war that lived in special camps and worked in the city.

I remember Fanny, a waitress, an attractive, simple country girl. Gentle, quick to smile, Fanny's brown eyes grew large with any childish excitement. Everyone liked Fanny. She met and fell in love with a French prisoner of war. The tall, serious young man cared a great deal about her. Their families tried in vain to discourage them. After a short courtship, when the war was over, they got married and left for France with Fanny's four-year-old daughter. As she was preparing to leave, she was torn between the love for her husband and the fear of living among the French people. Their centuries-old hatred of the Germans must have been especially strong then. Fanny kept repeating: "I hope I am doing the right thing, I hope."

* * *

Eventually, my work acquired its own routine. At 6:00 A.M. I began my day with cleaning men's and women's rest rooms on the main floor, and scrubbing the cement steps outside the entrance door. As time passed and my job went well, I became more confident. Before starting my work, I would dash across the street to the kiosk and buy a newspaper.

The Munich newspaper, one of the leading papers in the country, had no local news, no comics, no advertisements. It reported only national and international news. The newspaper had only four or six small pages. I could fold and hide it in the pocket of my apron. Since it was early in the day, most guests still slept. I went into the women's rest room and locked myself in one of the stalls. As I read the paper, I listened carefully. If someone came in, I quickly folded the paper and put it back into my pocket. I opened the door and pretended to have just finished cleaning the toilet bowl. With a hand brush and wet rags, I proceeded to scrub the sinks and the floor in the guest's presence. The men's rest room came next. The pail of water holding open the door usually kept everyone out. Occasionally a man would ignore my presence and walk in. I left quickly.

Usually fifteen minutes of reading the paper was enough to get the most important news. I saved the rest for later. I still remember how surprised I was to find all the information I craved. I followed the retreat of the German forces from the Soviet Union. The truth lay in print, though it was manipulated. It would say: "After a prolonged occupation, we pulled back from Smolensk for strategic reasons. We took along everything useful to us. We destroyed the railroad tracks, the bridges, and a good part of the city. The redeployment strengthened our position." Reading the daily newspaper became a must for me. I finally understood Father's passion for it.

After a while, a sudden fear rose in me. I wondered if I should be buying and reading the paper. Someone might see me and have questions. She knows German and is reading the paper every day? Why? None of the other Poles do it. Let's look into it. Should we notify the police or, better, the Gestapo? My imagination raced. This could lead to a disaster. I stopped buying the paper.

20

Herr and Frau Wittner owned the hotel. In her forties, Frau Wittner showed a great interest in her appearance and social status. She owned a stylish, expensive, custom-made wardrobe. She charmed her lady friends and the uniformed men in high positions. Her small, intimate parties hosted for select groups were quite successful.

She ran the hotel and made the decisions. Only occasionally did she consult her supervisors. The rest of the staff did not interest her. Rarely did I see a smile on her face, her voice had an unpleasant high pitch, and she was easily annoyed. At first critical of my work, she would watch me scrub the front steps and lament, "That's the wrong way. Didn't your mother teach you anything?"

I didn't want her to speculate about my background and put more effort into the scrubbing of the steps.

The labels on her suitcases came from all over the world, but recently she traveled only to German and Swiss resorts. Herr Wittner never went along. When she and Roger, who carried the heavy suitcases, walked out the front door, we all breathed a sigh of relief.

Everyone liked Herr Wittner. Quite a bit older than his wife, he was short, round, and walked with wobbly steps. Jovial, he had a good word for everyone. The hotel held little interest for him. Rumors had it that he inherited it and that Frau Wittner had been a poor, young woman, working in the hotel when they met. The Wittners lived in the hotel, and I occasionally cleaned for them. Frau Wittner's rooms were plush, had expensive furnishings, and lots of breakable souvenirs. I cleaned carefully. Herr Wittner's rooms upstairs looked like his refuge and showed his hobbies. Pictures of his hunting trips took up a whole wall. He and his buddies in Tyrolian leather shorts, felt hats with feathers, and colorful socks, displayed the bounty as their pedigree dogs cautiously sniffed the dead victims. A collection of rifles took up another wall. I had only seen rifles in the ghetto, in the hands of the German soldiers marching through the streets.

Birdcages took up the rest of the space. He had small birds and large birds, multicolored and dull. Two of my favorites, canaries, had yellow feathers and unbelievable voices. When they sang together, their tiny jittering throats released beautiful sounds like opera singers doing a duet. Herr Wittner had a name for each bird, knew its origin, age, and its favorite food.

Scrubbing the back steps of the Maximilian Hotel. July 1944.

Every morning he walked from cage to cage and carried on a tender conversation. The birds knew him and listened.

They didn't like me too much, however. When I opened a cage and put my hand in to clean it and give them fresh water and food, they would jump towards the door and try to escape. Their shiny eyes followed my every move. Before I left, Herr Wittner was quick to say, *"Sehr gut. Danke schön. Sehr gut."* ("Very good. Thank you. Very good.")

Herr Wittner seemed tolerant, a good human being. I had a feeling that I could count on his help if I should ever need it. But better not to need his help. Need no one's help.

* * *

What I liked most about my work was my freedom of movement. I didn't have to spend the whole day in one place. My job took me everywhere, and I became familiar with the hotel, the people, and their jobs. The smallest section—the laundry with only Maria and her helper. Tucked away in a remote corner of the basement, the best way to find the laundry rooms was to follow the strong smell of the chlorine, which irritated the eyes and the nose. When hot steam filled the air, I could hardly make out the shapes of the two washerwomen bent over the deep basins filled with hot, sudsy water. Mountains of soiled linens waited at their feet.

Since most of the washing and rinsing had to be done by hand, each load took hours to complete. At the end of the day, the two women were exhausted, their skin cracked and sore. I had only limited contact with Maria. I saw her only when I scrubbed the basement floor or when I needed a bath. Because only the guest rooms had tubs with hot and cold running water, the employees had to use the laundry tubs. Maria had charge of them, and when I asked to use one, her answer was always the same

"Again, you want a bath again? You just had one. I take a bath for holidays only and that's plenty."

We went through the same routine each time. She acted appalled. I just stood there, waiting. With great trepidation, she would reach for the pocket of her apron, pull out the key and give it to me. "Don't use all the hot water, and go easy on the soap," she admonished.

Maria, in her late fifties, was a tough countrywoman, used to hardships. She never complained, had great pride in her work and believed in the *Führer*. Hitler thrived on citizens like Maria, and I avoided them as much as I could.

* * *

The hotel kitchen, also in the basement, had a very different appearance than the laundry. Large and bright, the kitchen vibrated with the sound of chopping cleavers, banging pots and pans, and the chatter of the young women. At the long narrow tables, women peeled and sliced fruit and vegetables, rolled the sticky dough for the noodles, and ground the meat. Martha, the number two cook, supervised them. A huge stove with maybe twelve burners dominated the middle of the kitchen. Germany had no broilers at that time, but old-fashioned frying, roasting, and baking produced a variety of good foods.

The main chef and the boss of the kitchen staff—Herr Czerny. In his early sixties, he stood tall, had a dark complexion and limped slightly. Born and raised in Vienna, he made fun of the Bavarians and their dialect and disliked the Nazis. Outspoken, not even Frau Wittner contradicted him too often. Each cook had his or her specialty. Herr Czerny's fine touch and the aesthetic presentation, dressed the plates for special guests.

The lowest position in the rigid kitchen hierarchy fell to Hilde, the dishwasher. About the age of my sister and me, she had buckteeth, a strong lisp, and walked funny, most likely because of her bowed legs. Quite shy and eager to please everyone, Hilde washed the dishes in an adjoining, small room. She washed them all day long. Her apron always looked soaked and her hair matted. With red, rough hands, she washed and rinsed stacks of dinner plates, soup bowls, pots, and pans. The small, poorly lit, damp room gave off the bad odors of leftover food.

Hilde showed curiosity about Helka and me. We were the only foreigners she had ever met. She had many questions. I remember her saying, "I came from a village nearby, and I often feel homesick. How could the two of you have come from so far away and left behind your country and your family?"

We had no answer for Hilde.

Herr Czerny also showed interest in us. Strict and demanding, he didn't socialize with the staff, and his loud commands received instant attention. But he seemed friendly to me whenever I helped out in the kitchen. His name suggested a Slavic background. Before the First World War, most of southeastern Europe belonged to the Austro-Hungarian Empire, and many of their citizens were Hungarians, Czechs, Poles, and other Slavs. He knew we were Polish. The only other person he treated well was Bruno, his young apprentice. He liked his work and the *Hochdeutsch* (High German) accent. Rumors began to float around that Herr Czerny was homosexual.

The kitchen staff prepared three meals a day, with dinner served in the early afternoon. The squeaky old elevator, with pull ropes and a bell, carried the completed entree to the dining room on the main floor. The dirty dishes returned the same way. Even though poultry, beef, or veal, frequently appeared on the menu, the most popular dinner remained the traditional pork roast with potato dumplings. Oxtail soup and sauerkraut also had many followers. Various cakes and occasionally tortes—pies were unknown—seemed to be the favorite desserts. Besides beer, which every German loved, diners could select wine and Schnapps. Hotel food eaten by the guests far surpassed the fare of the hotel help or that of ordinary families.

I didn't want to think about what our father and Natek had to eat in the Forced Labor Camp in Piotrkow.

21

Only after I began to settle into my job and life at the hotel did I begin to realize who the hotel guests were. I had seen uniformed men in the dining room, ballroom, and the lobby. I assumed they visited friends, attended meetings or parties. I was wrong. All the hotel guests were military men of high rank. They lived there. At first, I couldn't distinguish one rank from another, but eventually the number of stripes on their uniforms and the salutes they received helped me to separate generals from colonels and the other officers. I wasn't sure which of them belonged to the Gestapo or Secret Service, or even if the hotel had been designated Regensburg's headquarters—but, Helka and I realized that we lived and worked in the midst of our most powerful and feared enemies. Since they occupied the whole hotel, I could not avoid them. If I had known in the beginning the identity of the hotel guests, I would have panicked. By the time I did realized who they were, we had lived there safely for some time, and the shock wasn't as great. I tried to stay calm.

Every morning as I scrubbed the cement steps outside the entrance door, uniformed men with chests full of medals walked right past me. Bent over, I could see the cuffs of their freshly pressed slacks and their shiny black boots. They carefully avoided the wet spots. These men would greet me with a friendly, "*Guten Morgen, Fraulein. Wie gehts?*" ("Good morning, Miss. How are you?") or the official "*Heil Hitler!*" with the raised right arm. They assumed I was one of many Christian foreign workers helping in the war effort. They almost rubbed shoulders with me, a Jew. A ready smile concealed my fear.

* * *

Several months after we started working at the hotel, I had an even a more scary encounter. I was vacuuming the large, beautiful ballroom after a well-attended party the night before. I slowly worked my way with the noisy vacuum cleaner from the back of the room to the front. An officer was reading and smoking a cigarette in one of the comfortable chairs. As I came closer, he motioned me to stop the noise. With a curious look, he asked me where I was from. "I have watched you work," he said, "and noticed the shape of your head, your profile and ears. I am an anthropologist with a special interest in the Jewish facial structure. Are there any Jews in your family?"

Panic filled me instantly. I thought, *Did I hear him right? What do I tell him? I better keep the panic out of my voice.* I said, "Jews in my family? Never. We never had any. What nonsense!" Without looking at him, I turned on the loud vacuum cleaner and continued to work. He still sat in his chair when I left the ballroom.

I went straight to Helka. Instantly, she could tell something was wrong. She stopped washing the cups and saucers, and we moved to a quiet spot. I told her what had happened.

"What do we do now?" she said. "Do we have to leave again? You know it's dangerous to run. We hardly made it the last time."

A waiter called for her.

"We'll talk later," she said. "I have to go."

* * *

I ran up to our room and began to analyze my face in the mirror. I couldn't see the shape of my head too well and only part of my profile, but my nose was of good size, even though not long or crooked. My ears were definitely large and somewhat protruding, especially the right one. I always had doubts about my looks. I removed the hairpins, which pulled my hair back, and let it fall freely. Hair now covered both of my ears. I studied my face again. Better, but maybe it was too late.

I had no way of knowing if the officer spoke to me out of scientific curiosity or if he might pursue the matter. If he informed Frau Wittner, she would know what to do. I didn't want to think about that. *Later, later, not now,* I told myself. I had no idea what to do. Helka seemed against leaving.

In the privacy of our room, we discussed what had happened again. "Did he seem threatening or just curious?" she asked.

"My facial features made him suspicious. I looked Jewish enough for him to ask the question. But he did smile, and he didn't follow me when I left. If I only knew for sure."

The expression on the officer's face kept coming back to me. But, comparing this situation with Neustadt, the threat didn't seem as serious or imminent. We did not run away.

* * *

By the summer of 1943, things seemed to be going well for us. The foreign workers in Regensburg, mostly Poles, Ukrainians, and Czechs, had formed their own social groups. After our experience in Neustadt, we tried to avoid Polish men and women. Though we had to wear the letter P on our clothes, we placed it so that a coat lapel or a scarf could cover it. No Pole in the streets would recognize us.

For centuries the Czechs had been known as the most enlightened Slavic nation. They had a strong democracy and an well-educated secular population. Their tolerance of minorities ran high, and we felt secure and comfortable with them. I don't remember how I met her, but Masha, a Czech girl, became my friend.

By the time I met Masha, my German had become quite good, and I read a lot to compensate for the loss of my formal education. At the local library, I took out books by Tolstoy, Romain Rolland, Goethe, and the Scandinavian writers. I even read Nietzsche, Schopenhauer, and other philosophers. Masha, a serious, intelligent girl, knew German well and also read a lot. Since Czech and Polish were related languages, we decided to use them. We each spoke our own language and understood each other quite well.

The two of us formed a mini book club. We would decide on a book, read it in German, write a review and discuss it in our own languages. Ibsen's *A Dollhouse* became one of our books. Because of the shortage of electricity, a flickering candle often lit our pages while reading.

(After the war, I told Masha that I was Jewish. "Oh, it must have been horrible," she said. "Where are your parents? Please, let's stay friends.")

* * *

Towards the end of the war, Helka met a young Czech man who fell in love with her. Well-educated and caring, he soon felt serious about her. She spent most evenings with him, and I waited up to hear everything about the date. My sister glowed. I loved her reports, and she did mine.

We both liked Louise, a waitress who worked with Helka, an attractive, coquettish young woman who smiled a lot and let us admire her dimples. Like most German women at that time, she craved a man. She quizzed my sister to know if she and her boyfriend were having sex. When she heard that they didn't go beyond hugging and kissing, she cried out in disbelief. "And he agrees to that? It's not fair. The young man is being tortured. I bet he is getting sex somewhere else. Why don't you send him to me? I won't take him away from you."

* * *

Joseph Wisnewski, a Pole, became my boyfriend. Shortly after I met him, I knew I could trust him. A few years older than I and an intelligent, compassionate, young man, he held socialist beliefs and cared about all human beings. I felt safe with him.

Joseph and I met frequently. After work he waited for me in front of the hotel. We took long walks along the Danube, went to the movies and to his sublet room. I liked the poorly lit room because he couldn't study my facial features too well. Even though I trusted him, neither Helka nor I would have dared divulge our true identities. Not to anyone.

Getting together with Joseph's friends made me uneasy, outright scared at times. They were educated Poles who blamed everything on the Jews and enjoyed anti-Semitic jokes. I had to watch my every word and gesture.

Joseph and I dated for over a year. My feelings grew strong and so did his. He became my first serious boyfriend.

Then a lively, chubby Polish girl joined our group. For a while, she tagged along, just another person included in our activities. Unexpectedly, Joseph began to see her alone. At the usual time, I ran to the hotel window and looked for him. He did not come back.

22

Roger, a French prisoner of war who lived in a POW *Lager* also worked in the hotel. Outgoing, well-liked and in his late twenties, Roger and I became the hotel's carpet cleaners. Outdoors, in the spring and summer, we pounded the handmade Persian rugs with a special carpet beater. After we released the thick clouds of dust, the lively colors and delicate designs came alive again. Even though Roger and I couldn't communicate too well, his German was weak and my French minimal, we understood each other. Our hopes were the same.

For quite a while, besides my sister, Roger, and myself, the hotel had no other foreign workers, except our roommate Else. Else, a chambermaid who cared for several guest rooms, had a medium build, reddish hair and an average appearance. When we occupied our room, she rarely joined us or pretended to be busy. Obviously she preferred to distance herself from us. Since she spoke German with a strange accent. I suspected that she was a *Volksdeutsche*—an ethnic German. The *Volksdeutschen* lived in Poland for generations and were considered Polish citizens. Before the war, they formed a small, hardly visible minority. After Hitler's occupation, they seemed to be everywhere. They spoke both languages, cooperated with the Nazis and wore German uniforms. They quickly gained power and took over many high positions and private businesses. Poles hated them, and Jews feared them. But I had no idea why a young *Volksdeutsche* woman would come to Germany to be a chambermaid in a hotel. In frank reality, I didn't know and didn't care to know. I only worried that she might find out who we were. Every morning, I tried to read her face. Had I given myself away during the night? Sometimes I talked in my sleep.

* * *

The spring of 1944—a year had passed since we had arrived in Regensburg, and our lives were good at the Maximilian Hotel. But I missed reading the newspaper. "What do you think, Helka, should I start again?"

"I am sure it will be okay," she said. "Nobody is watching you. Just don't stay too long in the rest room."

The next morning, I rushed back to the kiosk.

Without realizing it, I became overconfident and did some foolish things. Though the newspaper kept me well informed about the war, when Bruno, the young cook apprentice, invited me to listen to the London BBC news, I couldn't resist. He lived on the fourth floor in a single room, like the other employees. His window faced the window of a German family across a narrow alley. When I came in, he lowered his voice and said, "You are just in time. It's starting in couple of minutes." He shut the window, locked the door, kept the room dim and turned on the radio.

The broadcast began on time and came through clearly. The news, given in German, alternated in a man's and a woman's voice. Only some of the information seemed new to me, but it was the first foreign station to which I had ever listened and the first criticism and ridicule of Germany I had heard. Hitler's propaganda, delivered in his hysterical pitch, differed greatly from the calm condescension of the two British reporters. "Germany is not the mighty power taking over the world. Germany is collapsing." They finished the broadcast with a joke: *"Deutsche Luftwaffe hat mehr Luft als Waffe."* ("The German Air Force has more air than force.")

The program sounded great—a quick morale booster. When the broadcast ended, I sneaked out, looked around me and quickly entered my own room. Listening to the BBC had been a great experience—but too dangerous. It wasn't worth a long jail sentence. I never went back.

* * *

Another foolish thing I did was ask for a book. As my crew and I cleaned a room of a guest, I noticed an interesting book on the nightstand. When we finished the job, I wrote a short note. I asked to borrow the book for a few days and left my name. I expected the guest to be an older intelligent man, willing to share the book. I planned to check on it in a few days to find an answer.

The same evening, quite late, someone knocked on the door of our room. Helka opened it, and said with a surprise, maybe fear, "It's for you."

A fairly young, uniformed man stood in front of me. "*Guten Abend*," he said, "I read your note and came to meet you. Can you come over?" and he looked at me with a smile.

I didn't like the look or the smile. He did not mention the book. I declined his invitation and quickly shut the door.

*   *   *

The next, more than foolish, thing became complicated and dangerous. Herr Czerny, the chef, continued to be friendly to my sister and me. He chatted with us whenever he saw us. Irma, one of the assistant cooks, an attractive, young, single woman, was energetic, hardworking and loved to boss others. She seemed frustrated. Her ambition to advance on the job had been dashed because Herr Czerny didn't care for her. It made her envious that he showed friendship to the two of us, and she began to give me the worst jobs whenever I had to help out in the kitchen. She gave up her hope of promotion with Herr Czerny and tried to win over Ursula, the manager, and Frau Wittner.

Herr Czerny's interest in Helka and me grew and culminated in an invitation to go with him to Vienna. His vacation neared. He planned to go home and invited us to be his guests. We did not expect this and felt overwhelmed. "Take your time. Think about it, and let me know," he told us.

The invitation both excited and frightened us. "Why is he doing it?" asked Helka, "Can we trust him? What will the people in the hotel say?"

We went back and forth, back and forth. Not everyone in the hotel would know or care, and both of us definitely trusted him. He disliked the Germans, hated the Nazis and, as an Austrian of a Slavic background, felt close to Poles. And we had a hard time resisting Vienna, the famous city with its history and charm. We made a decision. We would go.

Herr Czerny took care of Frau Wittner's permission for us to go as well as the train tickets. Throughout the ride, he kept our tickets and our IDs. It was safer. The ride lasted a long time, but with the beautiful landscape, the time passed quickly.

Herr Czerny's apartment, where he lived alone, looked small, simple but comfortable. He made us feel at home. Because of his difficulty in walking, he stayed behind to visit with friends and family and advised us what to see in the city. Helka and I did the sightseeing on our own. We either took the streetcar or walked; we walked a lot. We visited the palaces, royal gardens, and museums, all of them spectacular. One day as we entered the Science Museum, I noticed a poster on the wall. Several people had stopped to read it. We joined in. It had descriptions, drawings, and photos of Semitic facial features. It claimed scientific proof. The anthropologist from the hotel came to mind. Helka looked at me and I at her. We moved away.

The wonderful week in Vienna passed too quickly.

*   *   *

When we returned, Irma's open hostility toward me escalated. She assigned me to a hard job outdoors on a cold, windy day. As I tried to explain to her that my own work, for which I was responsible, had not yet been completed, she shouted, "You refuse to do it?" and ran to Frau Wittner.

Frau Wittner made a quick decision: Irma was to take me to the police. With great enthusiasm, she marched me there right away. When we arrived at the Police Station, she didn't seem familiar with the building and walked into the first office. An older, relaxed-looking police officer gave us a friendly *"Guten Morgen, Frauleins."*

Irma presented her case. "She is a lazy Pole, gives me a lot of trouble and this morning outright refused my orders." She was agitated.

The police officer looked at me and asked a few questions. He was surprised at my German. I had gotten used to that. Most foreign workers could hardly communicate. I could tell his sympathy lay with me, not with Irma. He had me promise not to do disobey again and sent us back. Irma was boiling. I went to the kitchen, and she marched straight to Frau Wittner.

Frau Wittner showed up right away. She ordered me to follow her. As we left the hotel, I had to walk behind her. In her anger, she walked briskly, hitting the sidewalk with her high-heel shoes. As always, her suit looked elegant and stylish, her hair impeccable. I assumed we would return to the same police officer and followed her, keeping a distance. But we passed the police station and kept going.

I wondered where she was headed. Suddenly a large building with a red flag and a black swastika stood before me. I knew the building. It was the Gestapo Headquarters. Fear filled me.

She easily found her way and entered a room on the second floor. A stocky man in black Gestapo uniform, whom I didn't recognize from my previous visit, greeted her with "*Heil Hitler*" and a respectful "*Gnaedige Frau*" ("Gracious lady"). He must have known who she was. She gave him her most charming smile, pointed towards me and said, "She, the Pole, works in my hotel and has been disobedient lately. This morning she ignored the orders of a superior."

He glanced at me and listened to her attentively. As I stood in front of the heavy-set, calm man, I expected the worst. I could see him look up my record and find the soap coupon. The coupon had the name and address of the factory in Neustadt. Then he would find out that I ran away because I was a Jew. Arguing with Irma could cost me my life. My dry throat began to burn. I knew my fear showed in my face.

On her way out, Frau Wittner gave me a cold look and said to the officer, "Please send her back. Replacements are hard to get, and we need her."

What a relief. She wanted me back. But that didn't explain why she brought me to that awful place. As long as I remained in that building, the danger wasn't over. After she left, without looking at me, the officer went back to the papers on the desk, and let me stand there for what seemed the longest time. Finally he turned towards me: "If Frau Wittner has one more complaint, there will be punishment." The terrifying calm of his voice reminded me of the first Gestapo man I had met in that building. When he let me go, I had to force myself to walk, not to run.

A second miracle. I didn't need more warnings. I became cautious again and carried out any order given to me.

* * *

In my correspondence with Father, I made sure he knew nothing about those events. My once youthful father with whom I used to have a lot of fun. He liked to draw funny pictures for us, read aloud stories from the newspapers and played hard to get when he gave us the five *groszy* (cents) for an ice cream cone. My sister and I were about seven and nine years old, and what I loved the most was the candy ritual. In the evening, when Father closed the coal yard, he came home with a small, white paper bag. Helka and I knew what lay inside, and we rushed to greet him. The first one at the door got the bag. She could pick her own candy and distributed the rest. The round pieces of the semisweet chocolate had plum filling and the oval ones raspberry. Only Mother liked the milk chocolate

I never ate my candy right away. First, I inspected the size, shape, and texture, enjoying the way it felt. The richer, firm ones had a wonderful aroma. The mixture of strong chocolate and the delicate fruit tasted heavenly as it slowly dissolved in my mouth. I didn't hurry to swallow it. Frequently, on the way to meet Father at the door, the two of us bumped into each other, fell to the floor or ran into the wall. The candy was worth it. At that time, Father was mostly for the fun and Mother for everything else.

* * *

Now, Mother was gone. The Germans had torn her away from us. Father and Natek must have missed her. They still did. A dedicated partner to her husband and a tender mother to her little boy, she could have strengthened their hope and our courage. When I found myself thinking of her, I forced myself to stop. My eyes shouldn't look sad.

Helka and I lived and worked in Germany, our father in Poland. But we felt his presence. He took Mother's place. His letters told me that. He wanted to know every detail of our lives—where we lived and worked, the friends we made, the food we ate, and especially about our safety. More than once, he suggested we move to the country. He knew about the bombings. We practiced an art in our correspondence. To avoid the censor, we conveyed a lot between the lines. I destroyed all the letters as soon as we read them.

* * *

(Not too long ago, to my surprise, I found one of Father's letters—the only one that remained. The old piece of paper had yellowed and turned brittle. Parts of it had badly faded and become illegible. After more than fifty years, Father's handwriting with the small, round letters still looks familiar to me. I have a hard time looking at it . . . and thinking of him.

The fragile yellow letter, written in Polish, still brings tears.

Dear girls! May 2nd, 1944

A few weeks ago, I included only greetings to you, now I will write more. Tadek [instead of Natek] and I are still in the same place. We are both in good health and are getting by, as far as food is concerned. It's all thanks to Tadek. He is the one who supplies the extra food now, no matter how meager. Tadek, the twelve-year old, supports me. What an irony! You wouldn't recognize him. He grew into a handsome, daring boy. Even though our clothes, underwear, and bedding leave a lot to be desired, it can't be helped, it will not last forever. Sooner or later, there will be an end. One way or another.

Let me describe to you our daily routine. We get up at five A.M., to be at work at six. Our breakfast is bread, butter [Sara claims there was never any butter], and black coffee with saccharin [no sugar]. We eat the same at ten o'clock. [Early lunch?] Sometimes we have cooked food. I have learned a little how to cook.

Every Sunday, on our day off, Tadek and I go to church. I haven't read a letter from you in a long time. Are you still working in the same place? Could you possibly move to the country where it's much safer now?

[The following three lines are hard to decipher. The letter ends with:] I don't want to write how much I miss you. It's too upsetting. Many kisses to both of you, Bronislaw [instead of Bernard].

[In the line below, in big childish letters:]
Greetings, Tadek.)

Only once was I able to help them. Since the hotel provided our food, we received no coupons, and we couldn't buy anything. One afternoon as I was vacuuming the carpet in the dining room, I noticed something under the table. It looked like a wrinkled piece of newspaper. When I moved it closer to me, it turned out to be a booklet. A booklet bulging with food stamps. Some of them already had spilled to the floor; others seemed ready to fall out. I looked around, picked the booklet up and put it into the pocket of my apron. I feared the fat little treasure might still be visible. I put the vacuum cleaner in a corner and ran upstairs to our room to hide it.

I had never seen so many coupons for all kinds of foods. Helka and I were ecstatic. For the first time, we could legally shop in a German grocery. We bought canned meat, sardines, coffee and tea, cocoa, sweet condensed milk, and foods about which we couldn't even dream. We sent a large package on its way to Piotrkow.

23

I am not sure how the news trickled down to me, but I soon became aware that the year 1944 was not good for the Jews. The genocide continued, and the world remained silent. The Warsaw Ghetto Uprising the year before and the isolated, desperate resistance attempts suffered brutal suppression by German might. The sealed cattle cars continued to run on schedule, loading and unloading.

Luckily, the overall war situation improved. The Russians continued to drive the Germans back, inflicting heavy casualties. The underground movements in the occupied countries blew up railroad tracks, damaged strategic posts and killed German soldiers. The Allies had stopped Rommel's army in North Africa and forced them to retreat into Italy.

Everyone in Germany waited for the promised secret weapons. The streetcars, buses, and other public places were plastered with warnings: "Watch out, the foreign spies are listening in on the German civilians." A hateful-looking man with penetrating eyes glared at me from every placard. When the alleged miraculous V-1 and V-2 rockets finally hit England, that country did not collapse as the Germans had predicted.

And of course, the anticipated Allied invasion became a dark cloud weighing heavily over everyone. Private conversations, newspapers, and the radio filled with speculations, changing from day to day. Apparently the German military had been put on high alert. That made the civilians more fearful.

Several false alarms came. My long anticipation of a quick and successful attack on the Satanic German power wore thin. The war had already lasted almost five years and every additional day meant more suffering, more deaths. I knew that Father and Natek faced constant danger.

On June 6, 1944, a pleasant summer day, while I worked in the basement, as usual scrubbing the floor, I heard the announcement: The Allied Forces had landed in Northern France!

I ran to the radio. Herr Bauer, the headwaiter, had already shoved aside Fanny and Louise, the two young waitresses. My coworkers, Anna and Mina, stood next to them, and the kitchen staff rushed in. I didn't see Herr Czerny nor Bruno, his apprentice, and of course Herr and Frau Wittner must have listened to their own radio. Everyone in the crowded circle looked stunned. Some gazed out the small basement window; others stared at the cement floor. No one said a word. Maria, the laundry woman, who came in last, broke the silence: "The Americans and the British have landed in France? So what? Let them come. Our boys will take care of them." Only few paid her any attention.

I could tell that my presence made them uncomfortable. I left to find Helka. No one but she remained in her work place, and we hugged without words. I was sure the war would be over in a few weeks. The two of us would be back home in Piotrkow with Father and Natek.

It wasn't a few weeks. The war dragged on for almost another whole year. Meanwhile, life in Regensburg continued as before. *Hitler Yugend* (Hitler Youth) marched in the middle of Maximilian Street. Young boys followed their adult leader carrying a flag with the Nazi swastika. In their uniforms, neckties, and shiny shoes, straining their high-pitched voices, they sang: "*Deutschland, Deutschland, Uber Alles,* (Germany, Germany, above everything), *Uber Alles in der Welt* (above everything in the world). Today we have our homeland, tomorrow the whole world."

The children marched in goose step with exuberance and a sense of supremacy. They imitated the adult Nazis quite well. Hitler had hoped that they would secure his future.

But the men and women, passing on the sidewalks, no longer waved and smiled at the jubilant children. They kept walking at a faster pace.

*   *   *

In July 1944, a month after D-Day, a new event shocked the nation and probably the world. An attempt to assassinate Hitler. After some delay, the newspapers wrote about it. They described the place and time of the meeting. Pictures showed Hitler and high military officials sitting at a large conference table. It wasn't clear whether the briefcase with the explosives had been placed too far from him or if he had decided to leave the conference sooner than expected. Hitler, slightly injured, had survived. The young, distinguished-looking officer who had planned the assassination, had been tried, convicted and executed.

Again, as with D-Day, my hopes soared but soon crashed with painful disappointment.

* * *

It must have been obvious to the Germans that they were losing the war, the outcome only a matter of time. Neither the hotel guests nor my coworkers talked about it in my presence. I remember vividly one such incident. Frau Wittner was having one of her afternoon tea parties for her friends. As I came in, the ladies around the table carried on a lively discussion. They tried to predict who would occupy Regensburg. They feared the Russians, hated the French and didn't trust the British. They hoped the Americans would be the ones to take over the city. Before I began to serve the tea and pastry, as I had many times before, Frau Wittner grabbed the tray from my hands and sent me off. By then I had already overheard the discussion.

* * *

The bombs came next. For months, the German news media had reported the bombings: "The Americans and the British are focusing mostly on the civilians. They have destroyed schools, hospitals, and churches. They kill innocent women and children." Not a word about military targets. And, of course, not a word about the German atrocities committed in the countries they had occupied. We heard a lot about the bombings of Berlin, Leipzig, and Dresden—cities far away.

But, when the Allies began to bomb Munich, our situation changed.

Munich, the largest city in Bavaria about 100 kilometers south of Regensburg formed an important target. The American and the British planes came every day, and after a while I could tell them apart by their sound. At first, they flew over Regensburg on their way to Munich, and the loud siren came only as a warning. We didn't have to stop work, just pay attention. If we heard the siren again, that meant that the far away planes had changed their direction. Readiness was advised. A third alarm meant they headed towards Regensburg, and everyone had to seek shelter right away.

If the alarm occurred in the daytime, strangers streamed into the hotel basement from the street. Men, women, children, and elderly people looked for safety. After getting over their initial fear, small children often became restless and teenagers bored. The adults and the elderly took the situation seriously and didn't complain. Some alarms didn't last long; others seemed to go on forever. A few times, bombs actually fell on Regensburg, trying to hit two targets the allied bombers wanted: the distant factory of the famous Messerschmitt fighter planes and the railroad station. Because the station was located two blocks from the hotel, whenever the bombs fell over there, the hotel shook. Shattered window glass crashed to the ground, and a couple of times parts of the walls were ripped off. I don't recall any serious injuries.

Even though the night alarms brought fewer bombs, I hated them. They never came in the evening but in the middle of the night when I was sound asleep. At the first siren wail, I thought the alarm would end soon and ignored it. As the eerie sound continued, I knew what it meant. I had to get out of bed, take off the nightgown, put on my clothes (I never bothered to comb my hair) and run down to the crowded basement. Half asleep, I would sit on a folding chair, a box, or curl up on the cement floor. No one felt like talking; no one cared about his or her looks. I was curious about the generals and officers, whether, in the middle of the night, they looked as impeccable as when they walked down the cement steps in the morning.

I couldn't see any of them in the dark, crowded basement. If we were lucky, the screaming siren would soon let up, and I ran back to my room and crawled into bed.

I really hated the nights with several alarms. This was frightening and exhausting. At first, the moaning siren would became a part of my dream. It blended into the images in my mind, becoming either rumbling thunder in a storm or a powerful wind from far away. But as my sleep lightened, I recognized the eerie sound of the droning planes high in the sky. I tried to imagine a single bomber cruising in circles, positioning to drop its bombs on me, or a whole squadron slowly advancing towards me.

Half-awake, I recognized the air raid alarm. I knew I had to get up, get dressed and run for shelter. "Yes, I will do it. I will do it in a little bit. After a few more minutes of sleep." Sleep proved more powerful than my will. Every time I came to the surface of consciousness, a raw power pushed me back down. I kept bubbling up and down. Suddenly Helka's harsh, "Hurry up! Don't you hear the siren? We are the last ones on the whole floor. When you woke me up last night, I got up right away."

Helka was right. I knew quite well, that during the air raid alarm, to remain on the top floor of a large hotel, close to the train station . . . was stupid. It could kill us. And it wouldn't be the Germans but the Americans or the British.

Only long after the war did I get over the fear of the sound of a plane in the sky. Any plane.

24

A clear sign of the approaching collapse of Germany—refugees started coming into the city in droves. Military men as well as civilians tried to escape the quickly advancing Russian Army. And so did the Ukrainians, Latvians, and Lithuanians, many of whom collaborated with the Germans during the war. Refugees arrived in trains, buses, and army trucks. Before long, the East Germans became refugees as well. Their steady influx strained Regensburg's resources. The people needed food, housing, and medical care.

The women in the hotel talked about the refugees. Some showed understanding and compassion; others cut critical remarks. The newcomers looked somewhat different and often spoke with accents. Authorities forced some of the hotel women's relatives to take in refugees. This called to mind memories of our family being forced on others in the ghetto. I could still see Mother struggling with getting in and out through the window.

Even more shocking than the influx of refugees was the arrival of the soldiers. After conquering most of Europe, the once victorious German army looked a shambles, demoralized and frightened. Their ragged, torn uniforms made it hard to tell their rank or service. We saw many wounded ones with missing arms or legs, bandaged eyes or heads. The hotel became their haven. They slept on cots on the floor of the elegant, spacious ballroom, in hallways, and even on the wide, graceful stairway. I had to be careful not to step on sleeping soldiers when I came down to work in the morning. We found it impossible to keep the once elegant hotel clean. Frau Wittner wandered around, appalled but quiet.

* * *

Frau Wittner hired some of the refugees, two Latvian sisters, almost the same age as Helka and I were, among them. I remember them clearly. They and their family had escaped from Latvia with the German Army and arrived in Regensburg. The older one was assigned to my cleaning crew. Fairly attractive, with nice clothes, and an air of superiority, she knew that the two of us were Poles and looked down on us. The Germans had treated the Latvians much better than the Poles. She did not like her work; it was beneath her. "I never had to do that kind of work. My medical studies in Riga were interrupted, I had only two years left," she announced.

I couldn't stand her. My medical studies, about which I had dreamed for years, had never begun, and our war experiences were completely different. Throughout the war, the Germans protected the Latvians while exterminating the Jews. In October 1942, when the *Sonder Kommando* came to liquidate the Piotrkow ghetto, the Latvians arrived with them at the train station.

What I didn't know then but found out after the war—the East Europeans would be treated as victims of the German occupation. The Allies considered them displaced persons and housed them in the same DP camps as the Jewish Holocaust survivors. Even though some of them collaborated with the Nazis, they were even allowed to immigrate to the United States.

* * *

By the end of 1944, everyone knew that Germany would not last long. My sister and I still worked at the Maximilian Hotel, but we did manage to move. Father continued to worry about our safety because of the intense bombings. Frau Wittner, who needed more space for wounded soldiers, gave us permission to leave the hotel.

We were able to sublet a small, pleasant room from an older German woman, away from the train station and the military targets. Our room was located in the center of the old town, where the Sundays were especially pleasant. In the morning, I lingered in bed and listened to the resonating church bells of the old majestic Cathedral nearby.

Suddenly memories of Sundays before the war came back. Piotrkow had been peaceful. The church bells had rung, and the families streamed to the centuries-old Saint Bernard Church across the street from our coal yard. Father read the newspaper, and we played. When Mother, busy in the kitchen, announced: "Breakfast is ready. Don't let it get cold," the aroma of my favorite French toast, crisp outside and light and fluffy inside, got me out of bed in a hurry. A pleasant, lazy day had begun. A desire to be back there overcame me.

Few years, only a few years, and it seemed like an eternity since I had seen Mother in the kitchen.

The year 1935, when I finished grade school and attended the Jewish gymnasium, came to mind. The Depression still had wide-spread economic effects, and tuition fees stretched incomes. Father felt we couldn't afford it, but Mother insisted I continue. She gave up our maid, did all the housework herself and saved wherever she could. I still remember the dreaded mornings at school when the tall janitor with the cold, blue eyes, would appear at our class door. In a loud voice he would announce the names of the students behind on their tuition. My name was always on the list. I had to pack my books and leave. I couldn't return until the bill was paid.

* * *

Things improved when I got my first tutoring job. I helped earn the money needed. Fred, a nine- or ten-year-old boy, an only child, became my first student. The family lived close by in a nice, large apartment. Fred's mother had been Father's coal customer, and his father was our dentist. I think I was fourteen or fifteen when my gymnasium teacher recommended me as a tutor. At first I felt overwhelmed and didn't think I could do it, but both mothers boosted my confidence. I did the tutoring in their apartment under the watchful eye of his mother. I took my job seriously but couldn't believe that I deserved to be paid. Fred, a witty, likeable boy, had capability but little motivation. I saw his mother chuckle from behind the heavy drapes as she overhead the serious speeches I delivered to her son.

Fridays I would I run home and, with a pent-up voice, say: "Here, Mama, here is the money," and hand her the large silver *zloty*. It was the height of the Depression, and Father's coal yard could not support us.

25

With the extra money, Mother returned to her grocery shopping routine, and I went along whenever I could. Each week we took trips to several places. Milk, bread, and rolls didn't count. The baker delivered these fresh to our door every morning. On Friday, Mother and I would buy cheese, butter, and sour cream at the farmer's market. No expiration date needed—a farm woman had freshly made it. The chicken or goose, which we ate in the evening, had been alive in the morning. If Mother planned fish for the next day, it swam in a bucket of water until the time to cook it. With no chemicals available, fruit and vegetables all were organically grown and fully ripened in the sun. We had no refrigerators; we had to eat everything fresh. And we visited different stores for different products.

* * *

My favorite place—Mr. Gomolinski's small general store. Packed with goods, the shelves overflowed with non-perishables and the counters with fresh fruit and vegetables. Mr. Gomolinski laid out the freshly baked sweet rolls and my favorite cheesecakes on a small table. This store had been set up for frequent, quick stops. It was not always quick, however. Mr. Gomolinski, a chubby balding man could handle a store full of customers all by himself. While helping one person, he would joke with another and tease a third one.

"What can I do for you, my dark-eyed beauty?" he would say to a young woman, or "Of course, I have your special tea, Madame," to an older lady. If someone asked for rice and he didn't have any that day, he would carry on about the wonders of *kasha* and sent the happy customer on her way with a bag full of buckwheat. He never admitted to be out of anything.

I have never forgotten the butcher shop. Mr. and Mrs. Berg took care of the customers together. They knew all of them quite well. They knew who would buy the veal chops, roast beef, or the special cuts for meat loaf. Everyone bought his soup bones. Mr. Berg, a tall, husky man with strong arms and bloodstains on his white coat, conducted business seriously. His wife was the friendly one. She chattered with everyone while weighing and wrapping the meat.

The last couple of times I remember going into the store, Mrs. Berg attended it alone. Mr. Berg had not been feeling well. When we came again, Mrs. Berg anxiously asked Mother a question. Her husband had seen a doctor and was told that he had cancer. When Mrs. Berg asked if he would be okay, the Polish doctor had said, *"Ja Watpie."* With a worried look, she asked my mother what that word meant. Mother hesitated for a second. "It means, he will be fine."

In Polish, *Ja watpie* means, "I doubt it."

Though the weekly grocery shopping took time, it had its rewards. The store owners and the customers knew each other and their families. They often lived in the same neighborhood, attended the same *Shtibel* (small synagogue) and sent their kids to the same school. Their bonding lasted for years.

* * *

The Regensburg church bells continued to ring, but in my mind I still saw Sunday morning in Piotrkow. Mother, in a good mood, began to talk about her childhood. I loved her stories. After she had left Lukow, her hometown, she rarely saw her four sisters or three brothers. She missed them. Her mother had died young. I never knew her, but her Hebrew name was passed on to me. It is an old Jewish custom to preserve the memory of a loved family member.

Mother's father was a tall, broad-shouldered, mild man I found easy to love. During his visits, Helka and I crawled all over him, pulled and twisted his beard until we made a bunch of tiny braids. He loved it. We could never do that to our other grandfather.

Because of the expense of traveling, Mother rarely saw her hometown, family, or friends. Not much closeness existed between her and Father's family. The age difference, her background, and not keeping a kosher house kept them apart. I became aware of this as I got older.

The stories about her two daring cousins I found quite exciting. In the late twenties, one of Mother's cousins and his wife decided to immigrate to Palestine. He wrote that, on the way from Warsaw, his train would make a short stop in Piotrkow. Around midnight, my parents, Helka, and I went to the railroad station to see them. I was excited to be up at that hour. We waited for them in the dimly lit station. As the screeching wheels of the train stopped at the platform, a handsome, middle-aged man with a black, wide-rimmed hat and a beard stood in the open doorway with bright light falling on him. He called our name. Mother recognized him right away, and we went inside the train.

The short visit included many hugs and tears. Mother gave them jars of her homemade marmalade and pictures of our family. They promised to write often. After the shrill whistle announced their departure, I saw them wave at us until they dissolved into the night. On the way home, our parents talked about the cousin. "They had a comfortable life here in Poland and are leaving it for the hardships of Palestine. Where is Palestine and why are they going there?" Even I felt sorry for them.

Little did we know that a few years later my parents would envy the cousins in Palestine. They were out of Hitler's grip.

The next story was even more exciting. Mother's other cousin, who owned a large factory in Warsaw, worried about his son. Bronek, a bright student in his early twenties, had become a Communist. The Polish government considered the Communist party dangerous and declared it illegal, enacting severe penalties. At that time, Communism attracted some young, idealistic Jews with the promise of equality, a better life for the poor, and no anti-Semitism. They believed in the Communist ideology and joined the party, Bronek among them.

One day he came to his father's office as a representative of the factory workers. He demanded a pay raise and better working conditions. His father pleaded with him not to get involved, but he replied, "You are a rich capitalist. You exploit the poor workers." Bronek subsequently spent time in various prisons, even the one in Piotrkow.

Mother visited him, brought him reading material, food, and warm clothes. I wanted to meet this daring cousin of mine and begged Mother to take me along. She never did. A few months later, they transferred him to an unknown location. His father continued to bail him out until the money and connections no longer worked. This put Bronek in danger of being sent to Bereza Kartuska, a concentration camp for political prisoners in eastern Poland. The advice from the friendly high officials—send him abroad.

Bronek went to Paris and attended Sorbonne University. In 1936 when the Spanish Revolution broke out, he was one of the first foreigners to join in the fight of General Franco's Fascist Army. He suffered a serious wound and died.

* * *

As I got older, I noticed the differences among our family members. Our grandfather in Piotrkow was a *Hassid*, Uncle Sam a Socialist, and his daughter Hanka, a Zionist. Mother's family had also had Zionists, Capitalists, and Communists. Some grew wealthy, some stayed poor, some had secular educations, and others religious. I had no idea that, in the very near future, the rich Jewish life in Poland would be brought to an end.

26

When the spell broke, I returned to reality. Piotrkow slipped away from me. I still lived in Regensburg; the war still dragged on, and Danka and Mala's letters stopped coming. At first I assumed a short delay or misplacement of a letter. I wrote again and again—to no avail. No answer came.

Foreboding filled my mind. As Poles, Danka and Mala were less likely to face persecution. I worried that Father and Natek had had some trouble, that something had happened to them. Maybe, no longer in need of the wooden cots the Jews made for the soldiers, the Gestapo had liquidated the whole labor camp in Bugaj. Or was it the approaching Russians?

The end of the war seemed so close, and Father's last letter sounded optimistic. My mood sank, and I could not shake the fear. Each mental picture became scarier than the one before. I became listless, depressed and wanted to be left alone. Two comforting places brought some relief: the heavy brocade drapes in the ballroom, and the shores of the River Danube. I found the deep folds of the drapes a perfect place into which to escape. Whenever I could, I would rush into the ballroom and slip into one of the folds. The soft lining clung to my body, and the thick drape wrapped around me, creating soothing warmth. The blue, peaceful sky calmed me.

Walks along the river helped as well. Helka and I felt safer talking there than at work or even in our room. We kept asking each other the same unanswerable questions. "What happened in Piotrkow? Will we ever see them again?" My fear and pain intensified.

After a while, hiding in the folds of the drapes and walking along the river no longer helped. My desire to see the end of the war had vanished. The one who would have rejoiced at seeing Helka and me alive, and cherished every detail of our years in Germany, would not hear it. I feared that I would never see him or little Natek again, never hear their stories. The reunion I had hoped would come soon would never happen.

The briskly flowing Danube began to look inviting. I didn't share this sudden plan with my sister, but I contemplated jumping into the swirling water. I studied the deep waters and tried to imagine what it would feel like down there. The strong murky currents would bounce my body back and forth. Wet clothes would stick to me; the freezing water would fill my shoes and make my hair go wild. My lungs would fill with water before I could cry for help. A hidden power would force me down. I would thrash and fight, thrash and fight. No one would see or hear me; no one would help . . .

27

I did not jump. As 1945 began, I knew from the daily newspapers that the Russians and the Allies were advancing quickly and closing in on the Germans from the west and the east. I am not sure whether my coworkers told me so, or it was my own observation, but the Germans citizens had had enough. Enough destruction from the bombs, enough wounded and dead soldiers and civilians, and enough refugees. They resented Hitler's fanatical persistence. The Germans hoped for a quick end to the war and the American occupation. And, of course, all of us, the foreign workers, the POWs, and, most of all, the concentration camp inmates had high hopes. Lives depended on a quick end.

In this mood of growing anticipation, I experienced another shock. Early one morning, as I was scrubbing the front steps of the hotel, a group of about twenty-five to thirty men marched down the middle of Maximilian Street. They walked at a fast pace with armed soldiers at their sides. They wore the striped white and blue or white and gray prisoner's garments and were headed towards the railroad station. At first I assumed they were prisoners from the local jail, but something wasn't right. The men looked different. They looked emaciated and frightened. I ran inside to Helka and whispered, "I just saw a group of prisoners being marched to the railroad station. They looked like Jews from a concentration camp."

"How can you tell?"

"Well, look at them yourself. I am sure they'll be back tomorrow morning. They must be clearing the train station after the last bombing."

The next morning Helka saw them and agreed. An uneasy feeling overtook us. Within a few days, I knew their schedule. In the morning, they marched towards the station, and in the evening they marched back. I waited in front of the hotel and watched them. I tried to look closely at each man.

Suddenly a jolt: The man on the right of the third row looked like Father. I felt weak and dizzy.

He did, he looked like Father. I glanced at him again, but I could see only his back. I wanted to run after them but decided against it. The guards might get suspicious. I better wait. They would be back the next day. The next morning as they marched by us, Helka agreed. "Yes, there is a resemblance."

We were not absolutely sure. The man was not as tall and seemed somewhat older, but his build and profile did look like Father's. "But where is Natek? Why isn't he with him?" she asked.

"They could be together but working in different places." I said.

"That doesn't make sense. If they were together, why wouldn't they work in the same place?"

"You're always skeptical. Nothing's ever good enough for you."

"Well, you get excited too easily," she sneered and went back to the hotel.

My practical little sister was probably right. Maybe they should have the same job. But, I didn't want to lose my hope. At least Father or maybe both of them could be alive and close by. We should be able to find them.

* * *

In April of 1945 came the next shock. I worked in the basement cleaning and listening to the radio. The small basement radio, perched on a high shelf and left on all day long, had nourished me with important news. That day, as on many days, an announcer interrupted the program. "President Roosevelt is dead. The American president is dead!" a loud, excited voice kept repeating.

A few details of the place and time of his death came later. In no time, a large group surrounded the radio. Suddenly Hitler's voice came on. His hysterical shouting, after a long absence, seemed strange. He and Goebbels, the propaganda minister, painted a rosy picture. Roosevelt had died, and his close advisor, Secretary of Treasury Morgenthau, a Jew, would lose influence. Soon America would fall apart, and the Third Reich would win the war. This shocked me. Most of the listeners around me became excited and hopeful at this news. Once more, we stood on opposite sides. What looked like good news for Germans didn't sound good for us.

*   *   *

Up to this point, Regensburg had escaped serious bombings, but the air raid alarms continued. After we moved to the small room in the center of the old town, the basement of a nearby hospital became our shelter. We went there frequently. One evening as the two of us entered the shelter, we noticed Joseph's Polish friends with whom Joseph and I used to spend a lot of time. After a short greeting, Helka and I moved deeper into the shelter. As the skies remained quiet, even though the air raid continued, I walked up to the main floor.

To my great surprise, several of the Jewish prisoners whom I had seen march in front of the hotel lay in hospital beds. Jews in the hospital? Our Father might be among them. I wanted to get closer to look for him, but I didn't dare. I knew I faced serious risk in approaching them. If one of the Polish friends would go with me, it would be safer. Bolek, the handsome, not too bright young man, looked up to Stanley and followed his advice in everything.

Stanley of slight build and average looks was the self-assured leader of this small, Polish group. Intelligent, well informed and outspoken, he shared anti-Semitic jokes and also complained about the Jews in Poland before the war. "The Jews have always tied our hands. Whenever our government tried to pass a law they didn't like, the West European and American Jews spoke up right away."

As if the Jews in Poland didn't have enough quotas, restrictions, and blatant anti-Semitism.

I ruled him out. I decided to approach Irene, Stan's older sister. The motherly Irene, in her forties, was a heavy, good-natured, single woman whom everybody liked. She had always been nice to the two of us. I moved closer to her and said: "Irene, I just saw on the main floor several prisoners in the hospital beds. We have seen them walk by the hotel with the armed German soldiers escorting them. They look emaciated. They must be hungry. Do you think we should give them some food?"

She looked at me. "Them? I saw them too. They're Jews. Couldn't you tell?"

"No, I couldn't" I said, and walked back to Helka.

When the siren announced all clear, our Polish friends left, and I ran quickly to the main floor. I found the prisoners and the man I wanted to see. He faced the wall with his back towards me. I kept staring at his back and the half-bald head. I was so close to him, my heart pounded, and I couldn't move. My legs threatened to give out under me. I made myself go. As I reached his bed, startled, he turned around and glanced at me. He was not my father.

* * *

Hardly a couple of weeks after President Roosevelt's death, the American tanks reached the outskirts of Regensburg, surrounding the city. The rumbling shook the ground. At a frenzied pace, women bought all the food they could before the shops closed down. In plain view, Gestapo officers and their secretaries burned piles of secret papers on the sidewalks in front of their buildings. They didn't leave until these documents had turned to ashes. I would have loved to know what was in them. Lights went out, the streetcars stopped running, and frightened men and women ran for shelter.

As the sound of the oncoming tanks and heavy artillery grew louder, the city became paralyzed. An eerie stillness followed. The streets had emptied, and the bomb shelters filled. Our hospital shelter stayed packed day and night as the sirens moaned. Day changed into night and day again as we waited. I lost track of time and felt trapped among those strange Germans. They shared with each other sleeping space on the hard floor but not their scarce food.

I knew we had reached the final hours of the war. But the danger wasn't over yet. I feared house-to-house combat. Such action could easily involve civilians; we could be the victims of our liberators. We also feared that the Germans in the shelter might take revenge on us if they knew who we were. One look around was enough. These frightened and resigned people felt what we had on September 1, 1939, in our bomb shelter in Piotrkow.

The end came quicker than I expected.

Loud pounding on the door: "Its okay, You can come out . . . its over!"

A German woman, who just stepped out of our shelter, took up the refrain, "It's over. It's over!"

Helka and I whispered in disbelief. Then we rushed out. A long convoy of tanks and heavy artillery rolled slowly in front of us. Suddenly, from around the corner, a truck rumbled, packed with young soldiers in uniforms I hadn't seen before. The German men and women kept staring at them: *"Die Amerikaners, die Amerikaners!"*

Soon a loud "Hitler *kaput*, Hitler *kaput! Schone Frauleins!"* shouted the American soldiers. They whistled, waved, threw candy bars and packs of cigarettes to the young German women. Few waved back. Some watched in silence, but most of them turned away and left.

I felt like jumping up and down and shouting "You, boys, you did it! You risked your lives to free the world, to free the two of us. The nightmare is over."

I didn't jump. I didn't shout. I squeezed Helka's hand and tried to hide my tears. It was late morning, April 27, 1945.

28

The next morning a dancing streak of light found its way into my room. It came through the thin, lace drapes, hit my face and woke me up. *Still quite early*, I thought. *Didn't I cover the window with the heavy blanket last night? How could I forget the war routine of complete darkness because of the air raids? We even did it back home. But . . . wait a minute.* I suddenly remembered events of the day before. There would be no more sirens, no more bombs. The war was over. It had ended for us when the young American boys rolled into town.

I had waited almost six years, six long fearful years for this glorious day. *There should be celebrations and festivities*, I thought and ran to the window. Not even church bells rang, and no one sang or danced in the streets. It looked like an ordinary day in the town square of Regensburg. A shopkeeper struggled with wooden shutters before opening the heavy door for the long line of waiting customers. In the narrow streets, men and women walked briskly without a word. I saw a few noisy boys chasing each other.

No celebrations, no festivities. We were in Germany, among the Germans. Helka and I had to hide our feelings still.

Since Regensburg wasn't bombed heavily and the city surrendered quickly, I saw no major damage or ruins. But a few changes became obvious. The ever-present red flags with the black swastikas disappeared, and no single uniformed German could be found. Most propaganda placards vanished with a few left torn and swaying in the wind. No one sang: *"Deutschland, Deutschland Uber Alles, Uber Alles in der Welt."* Hitler's pictures disappeared.

The American GIs appeared everywhere. They weren't threatening at all. They behaved like civilians and looked like boys. What struck me most about them—their soft-soled shoes; I could hardly hear them walk. Not like the heavy boots of the German soldiers. Each time those boots hit the sidewalk or the cobblestones, the sound terrified me.

* * *

To my surprise, the guests of the Maximilian Hotel remained high military officials, but now they were the Americans. They took up all the rooms and set up some offices. The hotel could even have been the American Military Headquarters in Regensburg. I didn't know. No one would force Helka to wash dishes or me to scrub the steps and the toilets. Because we had saved most of the money we had earned, it would carry us through until we reached Piotrkow. One day, a young Dutch woman, a former hotel worker, asked us to help supervise the German women in the preparation of a party.

A banquet had been planned for the American generals and officers, and we were invited to attend. There were several of us: the tall blonde Dutch girl who was in charge and knew some English, a self-assured, attractive Russian teacher, and a striking, dark-haired Ukrainian who showed interest in the American men. Befitting the important occasion, the banquet was held in the ballroom.

The German women cleaned the Persian rugs, restoring their delicate beauty, ironed the white tablecloths and polished the sterling silver until it gleamed. The heavy chandeliers cast it all in a warm, intimate light. The dinner was elegant, with excellent food, wine, and music. Sizzling steaks, which I had never eaten before, replaced the German *Schweine Braten* (pork roast), large dinner salads took the place of the skimpy *Kopf Salat* (head lettuce salad), and the pies for dessert came as completely new to me. The mood was festive, and we all tried to look our best. I remember Helka and I wore identical dresses. The seamstress had sewn them out of drapes. We found the thin white fabric with a black vertical line perfectly suitable.

The officer who sat next to me, a young medical doctor, spoke fairly good German. He talked about the outpouring gratitude the French people had shown the American Forces and the slow and costly advance into Germany. We carried on a lively political discussion. I told him where I was from, how I survived the war and my plans to start medical school soon. It was a beautiful evening.

Couples filled the dance floor and, when the doctor asked me to dance, I became uneasy. The only dancing I had ever done had been before the war and in our kitchen. Guta, my high school friend, and I had tried the tango, waltz, and the fox trot again and again. The doctor could tell it right away how inexperienced I was and showed considerable patience. After a while, I caught on to the rhythm of the music and didn't step on his toes anymore. We danced for quite some time. As the music and dancing wound down, I noticed that the foreign women and their American partners began to disappear. They were leaving in pairs, hugging and kissing. The doctor looked at me and waited. When we returned to the table, I glanced at my sister. We both got up, said good night to our companions and left.

Because of the late hour and the curfew, we had to spend the night in the hotel. When we entered the room assigned to us, I began to panic. The room—downstairs, away from the guest rooms and near the hotel entrance—looked like a storage place with no key to lock the door. My sister and I worried that some of the men might try to come after us. After all, the two of us were alone, and they were men in a war that hadn't quite ended yet. And we knew so little about them. We pushed the sofa and heavy chairs against the door and took turns dozing off and listening.

* * *

All the languages I knew and used—Polish; the related Slavic languages, like Czech, Russian, and Yugoslav; German; some French; and even Hebrew and Yiddish—did not help me now. I needed English, and I didn't know a word of it. I could not communicate with my liberators, and I wanted so badly to talk to them. I found myself frustrated and envious of anyone who knew English. When Helka and I decided to turn in our false papers and reclaim our real names, we were sent to the CIA, the Central Intelligence Agency (called the CIC at that time). I had to find a German-speaking official.

With the CIA office located right in the hotel, we approached an American officer of German descent who spoke fluent German. I explained to this young, well-built man that my sister and I were Jewish, that we had escaped from the ghetto in Poland and had survived the war in Regensburg. We had false Polish papers and had been able to pass as Catholic Poles. We would like to obtain documents with our true names and return home.

"False papers? Who gave them to you, when, and where was it? Don't you know it's illegal?" He gave us a cold, suspicious look. "I will have to investigate this further. Come back next week."

I was shocked at the attitude of one of our liberators. We did not go back to him. A few days later, I found another CIA office down the street and decided to try again. I asked for someone who spoke German, and we were led to an adjoining room. Another young, uniformed man, of small build (I could not tell his rank) busied himself at the desk. When I began to tell him our story and the reason for our visit, he jumped up, exclaiming, "The two of you are Jews, Jews from Poland, and you made it? You survived the war?" He was beside himself. "I'd like to know more. Where in Poland are you from? What about your family? Were you in a concentration camp?"

I suddenly realized his excitement; this man, a Jew, had grown up in Germany. I told him that we worked in Regensburg, at the Maximilian Hotel. "How did they treat you? Did they pay you?"

I told him we had been paid, and I described the work each of us did. "The co-workers and the owner, Herr Wittner, were quite nice to us, but Frau Wittner took me to the Gestapo."

"To the Gestapo," he repeated in anger. "Why did she do that? Where is she now?"

Before I could fully explain the circumstances of the incident, he sent a soldier to the hotel to bring her in.

Within a short time, a smiling, well-groomed Frau Wittner entered the room. She hardly looked at my sister and me and proceeded with great confidence and charm towards the desk. I could tell she assumed that we were there to scrub the floors and wash the dishes and she to discuss the hotel accommodations. She greeted the CIA officer and introduced herself in English.

"Stand back," he hissed. "Do you know these two young women?"

She looked at us again, and still didn't get it. "Those two? Yes, they worked for me," she said and turned away.

The officer pointed towards me. "Did you take her to the Gestapo?"

She began to understand and muttered in German: "Yes, but they sent her back."

"They sent her back . . . but you will stay, stay in jail." The young officer called for someone. "Take her to the local jail and have her clean the toilets. I will call them later."

Frau Wittner looked mortified. She turned around and began to plead with me: "Please, forgive me," she begged in a shaky voice. "I'm sorry. I didn't mean any harm. Please don't let him send me there."

I began to feel uncomfortable. I had never been good at revenge, but the officer interrupted her with an angry: "Too late."

After they took her away, he wanted to know what else he could do for us and asked us to come back in two days. When we returned two days later . . . the officer was gone. They had transferred him to another location.

I never found out how long they kept Frau Wittner in jail or whether she really had to scrub toilets.

* * *

Sabina, in Regensburg, toward the end of the war.

The CIC officer's unexpected departure delayed the exchange of my false ID for a valid one. I don't remember all the details, but it seemed to take a while. I was anxious to be myself again. I had had enough of pretending to be a Catholic Pole and living in fear. I didn't want to hide my identity any more. But, as I looked at the small, worn document, I realized that without that piece of paper, the Gestapo would have shipped me to Treblinka with the rest of the Piotrkow Jews.

29

As soon as we received the new IDs, Helka and I wanted to leave. But it wasn't that simple. After the intense allied bombings, many large German cities lay in ruins. Power stations had been demolished, cutting the electricity, roads and bridges badly damaged, and no trains ran. We had to wait.

We did make a move from the small, cramped room in the old part of town. I went to the Housing Office, ran by the Germans but, like most of the institutions, supervised by the Americans. I told the German official who we were and what we wanted. The response floored us. With exaggerated politeness, he immediately checked his book and found for us more than I expected. The upper floor of a villa in a quiet, secluded part of town. He hoped it would be adequate. He even tried to assure me that he had known nothing about the Nazi atrocities. He had never heard of them.

The owner of the villa, who was either a banker or a business man, his wife, and an elderly mother treated us with equal politeness. They let us use some of their furniture for the bedrooms and living room and converted another area into a kitchen. They also had hated Hitler. We were to hear this over and over again in post-war Germany. *"Wir haben nichts gewusst. Wir sind unschuldig."* "We knew nothing. We are innocent."

* * *

Soon after, the first concentration camp inmates began to arrive. Germany had been full of forced labor and concentration camps. The survivors seemed to come from everywhere. Many of them looked dazed and forlorn. With their shaved heads—all camp inmates' hair had been shorn—they stood out. Some had such sunken faces and skeletal bodies that they required hospitalization. With my fluent German, I was able to help many of them. The sick men I took to the hospital, and I found rooms to sublet for the stronger ones. Because the Americans kept a close eye on all German institutions, no one dared deny the survivors hospital admission or a sublet room. I made many visits to the hospital and the Housing Office.

* * *

Unexpectedly one day a Jewish-American GI arrived in his jeep and asked if he could help. I don't know how he heard about Helka and me, but he became our angel. As more and more weak and bewildered survivors showed up, this GI, whose name I have long forgotten, but whose photo I still have, kept delivering food and clothes from the Army with the permission of his superiors.

Helka and I with the Jewish-American GI who supplied food and clothes for the survivors. Early summer 1945.

His family lived in New York. He had learned Yiddish (similar to German) from his grandmother, who grew up in a *shtetl* (a small town in Eastern Europe). We communicated with each other without knowing English. We were comfortable with him, and he felt a part of us. From his Jeep, either alone or with a friend, he would unload Spam, tuna, cigarettes, and candy one day, shoes, slacks, and shirts another day. The needy survivors thrived on all of it, and our villa became an unofficial relief center. As time went on, the arriving survivors looked in better physical health but were all driven by the same desire: to find their families. The Germans had torn them apart at different times, in different places. Because nothing was or-

138

ganized, this search proved difficult and frustrating. Only word-of-mouth information or handwritten lists were available. Survivors would stop other survivors, even if they didn't know them, and ask the same questions: "Where are you from? What camp were you in? Have you seen or heard of ____?" and they would pass along the names. The long lists, which hung in many town halls, helped only a little. The survivors would write their own names and the names of the relatives they hoped to find on these lists. Only occasionally a happy outcry came from the somber crowds. The searching men continued to travel from town to town mostly in the trucks that transported the American GIs. They would stop every stranger, read and sign every list. Even though this method had meager results, no one was giving up.

* * *

And neither did Helka nor I. Our wounds were fresh. Even though, most likely, Mother had perished, I had no proof. I carried a glimmer of hope.

Jewish boys and teenagers out of concentration camps—some of the many I helped. Regensburg, summer 1945.

It was quite different with Father. The correspondence between him in Piotrkow and us in Regensburg gave me the illusion of being together. I had a picture of his life, no matter how terrifying. All his letters had been full of love. He had watched, advised and tried to protect us from afar. None of us could reveal it, but we had made plans. Plans of our new life together. Every day apart added to my fear.

I would ask every survivor who passed through our relief-center villa. "What town are you from? (Most of them came from Poland.) What *Lager* were you in?" and then give them the names, ages, and descriptions of our father and brother. They tried to help, but often the information we received proved either inaccurate or mistaken. We only knew that Father and Natek had been together in Piotrkow until the end of 1944, when our correspondence had stopped. No one could tell us for sure what had happened to them after the Germans liquidated the Bugaj labor camp. One day, someone would say that he had seen Father and Natek in one concentration camp, and the next day someone else said they were in a completely different one. Upsetting. I dreaded their silence even more. I was not giving up.

The first reliable news came from a man from our hometown. He knew Uncle Sam and told me that our uncle had survived in Buchenwald. He had seen him there. The same man had heard that our uncle had left for Piotrkow. My hope rose. Since Father and Uncle Sam had been at the Bugaj camp together, they must have been sent to the same concentration camp. Uncle Sam was older and frail; if he made it, Father and Natek surely had lived and most likely had also returned home.

* * *

By then Helka and I had heard the horrible stories from the inmates who had survived. They had witnessed the atrocities of the concentration camps: the hunger, beatings, the dreaded selections, and deaths. So many died every day. They talked about the gas chambers, the crematoria, and the foul smell of the burned flesh rising from the chimneys. They kept repeating the horror stories over and over again. At first, I couldn't believe it, then I couldn't listen. I almost felt guilty about my easy two years in Regensburg.

The roaming survivors brought good news also. JOINT, the American Jewish Relief Organization, had set up an office in Munich and began to help. They provided food, clothes, and shelter. They organized and improved the search for the relatives and began the emigration process. They opened DP (Displaced Persons) camps to give the survivors a place to live. The DP camps sprang up everywhere in the American zone (the part of Germany occupied by the American Forces). Former concentration or prisoners-of-war (POW) camps became DP camps. Some of them even retained the barbed wire and the armed guards. The American military had no experience dealing with civilian refugees and treated them as if they were prisoners of war. The DP camps provided housing, food, and clothing but were crowded and had poor sanitary conditions. Not until Eleanor Roosevelt, and later General Eisenhower, visited the camps and reported the depressing situation to President Truman, did conditions change. The improvement was drastic. If I remember correctly, some camp inmates, Jews among them, requested and were given permission to live with their own people. Because of bad war memories, Jewish survivors preferred to stay away from the East Europeans.

* * *

As the survivors continued to pass through Regensburg, I noticed few women among them. Apparently women either perished before being sent to concentration camps or, once there, didn't live long.

From the hundreds of men I saw, two remain in my memory. One man, in his late twenties, with shaven head and old and worn *Lager* garments, said, with tears in his eyes when he first saw me, "You are the first Jewish woman I have seen since the liberation. I didn't think I would ever find one." When he left to continue the search for his family, he gave me his picture and wished me success in finding my dear ones.

The other survivor, who also left me a photo, was Ben, a fourteen- or fifteen-year-old, tall, attractive boy, the only one of his family who lived. He had sad, brown eyes and clung to Helka and me for quite some time. A while later, when Ben came to say good-bye, he wore shoes, slacks, and the shirt of an American GI. Only his cap looked civilian. His face had filled out, and his eyes had a serious, determined look. The American officer, for whom he had worked, had arranged for Ben's early emigration. He was leaving for the officer's hometown, somewhere in America. I often wonder what became of him.

At that time, it was hard to keep track of one another. Everyone lived in a state of transition and remained so for quite some time.

141

30

I grew impatient for our trip back to Piotrkow. The war had ended more than three months before, and still we waited in Regensburg. Signs of the huge devastation of Germany slowly vanished as teams of workers gradually removed the ruins of demolished buildings, restored electricity and repaired roads and bridges. Crowded trains still faced lengthy detours and layovers and never ran on time. But they ran.

* * *

Of the millions of foreigners, with various looks and languages, whom the Germans had forced to work in their country, only a few had managed to leave. Forced workers and POWs from France, Italy, and other West-European countries, numbered in the first to go home. Their homelands had been freed, and their families waited.

The Czechs, Poles, Ukrainians, and other East Europeans had also come as workers—some forced, some voluntary. The Jews had spent time either as inmates of forced labor camps or, most often, concentration camps. While West Europeans quickly boarded trains to go home, the Czechs, Poles, and the others hesitated. Though many of their families had survived the war and the refugees suffered homesickness, they feared the Russians and their Communist regime. The Jews, however, faced harsher times. They had lost everything. No families waited for most of them, they could not recover their properties or businesses, and the Poles didn't want them back. I heard this from many survivors. The Germans had confiscated their possessions at the beginning of the war, and the Communists refused to return them after the war. They didn't allow private enterprises. Since the emigration process, unlike repatriation, lagged, many Jews spent years in the DP camps. Even though people considered life in the camps to be temporary, marriages occurred and babies came. Many newborn babies. As if new life could fill the huge gap the Nazis had left.

Quite a few survivors preferred to live outside the camps and settled in Regensburg. The needs of the growing community required more than what we could provide from our villa. Several capable survivors approached the two of us. "Since you were the founders of this relief center," they said, "would you join us in forming the Jewish Council we need now?" We couldn't. The trip home had become our first priority.

*   *   *

Richard's brother, I forgot his name, decided to join us on the journey. Richard had been a member of the Sanitary Service during the typhus epidemic in the ghetto. I met him shortly before the liquidation and kept thinking about him. I even mistook a stranger for him in Neustadt once. His brother, as was the case with many other survivors, just wandered through Regensburg in search of his family. When I saw him (I think he had come to pick up some food parcels at the villa), I was shocked. I recognized him and assumed that Richard had come with him. But he hadn't. He didn't know my father or Natek. He was searching for his girlfriend, his mother, Richard, and his youngest brother. In the last few months of the war, the Germans had separated his mother and her three sons, and Richard's brother still had not heard from any of them. Since he wanted to return to Piotrkow, he agreed to travel with Helka and me.

Many people advised my sister and me not to travel alone. The destruction and chaos all over Europe made it unsafe for two young women to be on their own. Finding Richard's brother came as a big relief to us, and, after short preparations, we were on our way.

With destruction all over Europe, the trip proved more difficult than we had expected. We did a lot of hitchhiking, mostly on the U.S. military trucks, and quite a bit of walking. The trains had not improved, did not arrive anywhere on time, made long stops and detours. It took days to reach any destination, and anxious masses packed every station. Food, either from the vendors or travelers' bundles quickly disappeared. We had to push and shove to get a seat and didn't dare leave it afterwards. Sleeping bodies covered the floors. People even rode on the roofs of trucks and trains or hung onto the outside door handles. Richard's brother made a great companion. He was a broad shouldered, muscular man in his late twenties, with only a slight resemblance to Richard.

I don't remember how long it took to travel from Regensburg in southern Germany to Piotrkow in western Poland. As we approached my hometown, I became nervous. I had left when I wasn't quite twenty and returning at twenty-three—only three years, but so much had changed. I feared to face those changes.

*   *   *

Arriving in Piotrkow gave me an eerie feeling. The streets, parks, buildings—the whole town—looked familiar, but it felt distant and strange. At first I couldn't tell why, but it didn't take me long to realize the difference. Our people were missing.

Uncle Sam and his daughter Sara had survived and returned, and we had no trouble finding them. The three-story apartment building in which they lived looked old and neglected. Though the outside walls had grayed and peeled and the inside looked messy, the building was packed with young families. Mothers yelled at their children, who ran barefoot up and down the steps smudging up the walls, while teenagers, cigarettes in their mouths, pushed them aside.

I found Uncle Sam's apartment on the main floor. At first I hesitated to knock on the door, fearing the news I would learn, the news I needed to know for so long. My fear rose. But, finally, I knocked. In the loud "Who is it?" I recognized Sara's voice. She used two keys to unlock the door. When she opened it, we just stared at each other. For a long moment, no one uttered a word. Then the three of us laughed and cried, laughed and cried. Finally we remembered to hug. Uncle's voice came from the living room: "Sara, who is it? What takes you so long?" He sounded annoyed.

"Father, come and see for yourself!" said Sara.

A heavy chair skidded on the floor as he pushed it aside, and, with a hardly audible grumble, Uncle entered the hallway. He stopped at the threshold: "Oh, my God!" he cried out in Yiddish. "It's Sabka and Helka! It's them! I have to sit down."

As we followed him into the living room, he told us, "I know that Natek is alive in France. I'm not sure about your father. Let's talk tomorrow." And he left the room.

"Your uncle isn't the same, but you must be tired and hungry. Let me fix you something," Sara said and disappeared into the kitchen. I could hear the teakettle on the stove and the banging of the cabinet drawers. I wasn't hungry. Helka and I nibbled at the sandwiches she made for us. Sara fixed our bed, and the evening ended. I tossed and turned during the long night.

Uncle and Sara had changed a lot: he had aged visibly, his once straight back had become stooped, and he looked thin. His cheerful disposition had vanished. Sara's shaved head shocked me. I had seen many shaved heads on the survivors, but hers bothered me the most. She had been so proud of her wavy, blond hair, and it was gone. The few stiff hair stubs pushing their way through her naked scalp would need a long time to grow back. And she was also thin, very thin.

The apartment appeared dingy and depressing. The sparse furniture looked old and worn, and they had no bathroom. Before I went to bed, Sara had to go with me to the outhouse. I could smell it from far away.

The next morning Uncle Sam told us what he knew. He said that during the war, as a member of the Jewish Council in the ghetto, he knew of the huge losses devastating our extended family. He knew, but he couldn't save anyone, not even Hanka, his youngest daughter. He knew of our mother's arrest, her detention in the synagogue, and the cattle car to Treblinka. No one had heard from her since.

But he still wanted to remain in Piotrkow. "I came back because this is my home," he told us. "I belong here. I will open a tailor's shop and get back to a normal life."

"Normal life," cried out Sara. "It will never be normal again. It's not only that my mother and Hanka are gone. We would be the only Jews in Piotrkow."

"That's nonsense," my uncle protested. "Jews are arriving every day."

"Yes, they arrive every day, but they leave a few days later. Felix and Arthur [two married cousins, who lost their families] are gone. You couldn't convince them to stay. They have heard about some Poles attacking the returning survivors, especially if they tried to claim their pre-war possessions or businesses. Nothing has happened to us, but why wait?"

After breakfast, Sara reluctantly began her story. "It was the end of 1944 when they took us away. The Russians were already in Poland, not too far from Piotrkow. The Germans quickly liquidated the Bugaj, our forced labor camp, separated us from the men and sent us to various concentration camps in Germany. Mother and I ended up in Bergen-Belsen, in northern Germany. The place was terrible. People were dying all the time, and they threw the corpses into a big pile. Hunger, TB, typhus, and dysentery were killing us. The two of us were extremely weak and skeletal but survived.

"The British Army liberated us and tried to help. The soldiers gave us their food—canned meat, tuna, chocolate—the best they had. I had warned mother not to eat too much of the rich food. But one day when I left her for a short time, she could not resist. Mother ate a whole can of Spam. Her diarrhea got worse, and she died the next day. Why did I leave her alone?" Her voice broke.

Hesitantly, Uncle also talked about the last day at Bugaj. "They sent your father, Natek, and me, with many other men, to Buchenwald, a concentration camp deep in Germany. The inmates of the large camp, a lot of them Jews, came from various countries."

Uncle didn't know then, but Buchenwald was one of the first concentration camps Hitler had build shortly after he came to power. He sent the German Socialists and Communists—his political opponents—there and kept them for many years. During the war, the Gestapo treated the German prisoners better and used their help in running the camp. Gradually the Socialists and Communists gained power and formed a strong underground movement. They showed compassion to the Jewish inmates, especially the children. They gave the children better quarters, more food, and advised them when not to obey the Gestapo's orders.

"I couldn't talk about it last night, but, for a short time, Natek hid your father and me in the children's barracks. We all knew and especially Bernard, who always had the latest news, that the end was near. One day he said to me: 'Sam, I know the American Army is nearby. The war is over, next week we will go to Regensburg to get the girls.'"

Uncle Sam had to stop. It took a while before he could continue. "In the last few days, the Gestapo was frantically rounding up the Jews and sending them on a death march. Hardly anyone returned. Around noon, when Natek went to look for food, he warned your father not to leave the barracks. But Bernard couldn't live without the latest news. He said to me. 'I am going only for few minutes. I will be right back,' and he left.

"We kept waiting for him. He never came back. Two days later the Americans liberated Buchenwald." Uncle's eyes tried to avoid mine.

* * *

Father's image stayed with me for the longest time. I refused to believe the news. Nobody saw him die. He could have escaped. People still arrived occasionally. He might too. He was in my dreams. I could see him by himself, and I could see him with Natek. Through the miseries of the ghetto, the forced labor camp and the concentration camp, he had stayed alive for us. Because of Natek, he made it from day to day, and because of Helka and me, far away, he clung to life even more.

His image became most vivid in Buchenwald. He looked older than his forty-seven years. I imagined him in worn and dirty clothing, his thin hair almost gone, his face sunken, but his eyes watchful. The aching bones and gnawing hunger didn't matter. He believed that he had made it. For him, the war was over, and he relished every detail of Germany's collapse. Every detail of the news counted. He had been like that all his life.

He didn't have far to go as he sneaked out of the barracks for the news. In my mind, I saw two Gestapo men appear suddenly out of nowhere. He had no place to hide, no time to think. When they forced him into a death march with other men, he tried hard to stay in step. Every time an outcry followed a bullet, he walked faster. I could almost hear him cry out for us as he fell to the ground.

The news about Natek sounded both good and bad. He had survived, but he was in France. Uncle Sam said that, after the liberation, chaos continued in the camp, and inmates continued to die. The war still raged in neighboring towns and villages. After Germany's official surrender, Natek and other boys, Eli Wiesel, and Rabbi Lau (chief rabbi of Israel), among them, were declared war orphans and sent to various countries. Natek went to France. Uncle Sam didn't know where. The thirteen-year-old boy, alone in a strange country, had just lost his father, whose love had protected and nurtured him during those terrifying years. They had been inseparable. It must have been devastating.

Helka and I decided to try to locate Natek and bring him back.

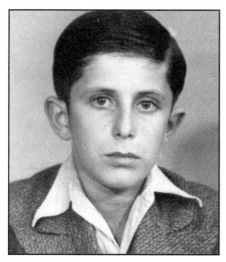

Natek, after the liberation, spring 1945.

Piotrkow, September 1945. Sara, Felix, Helka, Uncle Sam, Sabina, and Arthur. Natek still lived in France. Survivors of a family of over fifty relatives.

31

I had heard enough. Nothing held me in Piotrkow. Father's coal yard lay as an empty strip of land, and a strange family lived in our apartment. Instead of warm greetings, stares came my way. A cold wind whistled through the empty streets of what once had been the Jewish part of town. Even though our immediate family never lived there, I still felt connected. That's where my grandparents, aunts, uncles, cousins and many of my friends had lived. I knew the narrow streets, the old buildings, and the small, crowded stores by heart. They had vibrated with life. On my way from school, I could hear the customers bargaining, the shoemaker pounding the soles, and the barber whistling while he cut hair. Mrs. Goldstein's pastry shop used to lure me inside. With my five or ten *groszy* (cents), I could choose a donut, without a hole and filled with jam, a slice of the rich, moist cheesecake or any of the various cookies. I had a hard time deciding. With the pastry melting in my mouth, I passed the Jewish men and women rushing in all directions and the kids who played and shouted on the crooked sidewalks and bumpy cobblestones.

But that was then. Not even three years later, only silence, a penetrating silence remained. Occasionally a man or woman would cross the street or a stray cat lick her paws on an empty sidewalk. The buildings remained, but our people—young and old, rich and poor—were gone, gone forever. I couldn't take it. I did not want to see the apartment building where our grandparents and the five of us had lived in the ghetto, the street where Hanka and I took our walks and discussed books or my gymnasium where I spent the last four years of the prewar time.

I had just realized that out of our extended family of fifty to sixty people, the cousins Felix, Arthur, Uncle Sam, Sara, and the three of us, Helka Natek, and I—a total of seven—were all who had survived. Out of my mother's even larger family, I knew only of our cousin Paul and his sister Pola who remained.

In Piotrkow, as in all other Polish cities, towns, and villages, the Germans had killed ninety percent of the Jews. Ninety percent! Poland, had become a huge, invisible Jewish cemetery.

* * *

A few days after our arrival, Helka and I went to see the Justyna family. As we approached their villa at the outskirts of town, I noticed the small, wooden shed. The night terror of the ghetto liquidation came back in a flash. Again I could hear the screams and the gunshots. Again I felt that sharp loss as our lives changed forever.

The large, comfortable house showed little change. The rooms looked spacious, the kitchen bright and warm. The ladder to the attic stood in place as it had when we used it.

Only Mala was there to greet us. We had the tearful reunion for which we had waited all the years of the war. Even though we had corresponded for a good part of the war, a lot of important news had to be left out. Mala had the answers to the questions we had not dared ask before.

In the fall of 1942, their mother was able to give us three sets of false papers, though we had asked only for one, because they themselves already used false identities. Mrs. Justyna, her two daughters, Danka and Mala, but not Mr. Justyna, were members of *Armia Krajowa* (the Home Army), a Polish underground movement. Danka smuggled weapons, and Mala passed secret messages. They traveled a lot and faced constant danger. They carried cyanide poison to use if captured by the Germans. Mrs. Justyna ranked high in the movement, and their home became an important meeting center. National leaders met and frequently stayed in their house.

"The reason Mother told the two of you to leave was because a house guest, a member of the underground army had discovered you. That was in late 1942. Two years later, the Gestapo arrested, tortured and sent Mother to a concentration camp in Germany. Danka and I immediately left home, and we remained in hiding until the end of the war."

"Was it then that you stopped writing to us?" I asked.

"Yes, that's when we had to stop the correspondence."

"In January of 1945, the Germans caught Danka and kept her in prison in Czestochowa. While awaiting her death sentence, the Russians liberated her, and she returned home. But Mother hasn't come back yet." Mala's voice began to quiver. "Right after the war, because of her poor health, they sent her to Sweden, and she is still there." Danka had recently married her superior in the underground movement.

"Oh, I almost forgot," said Mala, and she rushed out of the room. She came back with our mother's silver Shabbat candleholders. They had been in her family for several generations. Mother had left them with Mrs. Justyna before escaping the ghetto. She planned to light the Shabbat candles again.

The Justyna family, as many other Poles, had suffered considerably. Early in the war, a German soldier had shot Yurek, the epileptic son, who ignored his order to stop running. The parents found him dead in front of their house.

After we had caught up with what had happened in the Justyna family, Mala had questions about our three years in Germany. We told her how we had fared and the dangers we had faced. We had a hard time parting.

* * *

Shortly before leaving Poland, I visited Lodz, the large city nearby, and found Julius, the friend from the Ghetto, in whose apartment our small group used to meet to discuss books. Julius was the one who gave me the courage, a few days before the liquidation, to use my false Polish ID. He himself had survived on false papers.

In the summer of 1944, he fought in the Polish uprising in Warsaw. Now, after the war, he and his wife studied at the university. Julius continued to use his false papers. We stayed up late one night and compared our war stories. He tried to convince me to remain in Poland: "This is the country you grew up in. You know its culture, the literature and language. You will never reach the same level in another language as you did in Polish. Wherever you go, you will be a foreigner with an accent."

"Yes, you are right," I told him. "My new language will not bring me to my previous level, but I won't have to hide my identity. I don't want to pretend to be a Catholic Pole any more. I am a Jew. And I am not welcome here."

32

Leaving Piotrkow turned out to be more difficult than I expected. The required documents had to come from the city hall. Obtaining these papers proved less than a simple matter. It took many visits, pleading, and finally bribes.

At last the four of us, Uncle Sam, whom we had to convince to leave, Sara, Helka, and I boarded the train. We headed west to Germany, back to Regensburg. People crowded this train just as the one into town. It again took a lot of pushing and shoving to get in. We looked for Richard's brother, but he must have left already. After a few hours on the train, an uniformed Russian made his way through the crowded aisles. I had never seen Russians before. This man, a young, cheerful soldier with his cap pushed back, joked with the young women as he collected the documents from all the passengers. As he reached us, in a loud, cheerful voice, he announced, half in Polish, half in Russian, "Papers, ladies. I need your papers," and smiled at us. He took Helka's first and put them in his black bag. After he took Uncle Sam's, Sara's, and my documents, he began to grumble that the bag was full and shoved them into his pocket. By then the train had sped up, making good progress.

About half way through the trip, we had to change trains. We found no seats or standing room inside the cars. Only the roof had some space. The four of us had to climb up. A couple of husky men lifted us off the ground, and someone's strong arms pulled us onto the roof. Even that space had near-ly filled. Groups of people huddled together. At first I feared sitting so high up and in the open. I could see myself being thrown off if the fast train should take a sharp turn. But I relaxed when I saw everybody else at ease. I put on a scarf to keep my hair from blowing and began to enjoy the mild September day. I looked forward to watching the stars at night. It was early evening, and the train hadn't left as yet, when a burly Polish man climbed up on the roof. His hair looked greasy and matted, his clothes covered with coal dust, and his breath smelled of vodka. He landed next to us. With a front tooth missing, he smiled and mumbled something. He faced Helka. "You, you come with me to my office," he said and pointed toward a small shack tucked away on the other end of the platform. "I have to check your papers."

Helka tried to move away, but he grabbed her arm and began to pull. The three of us—Uncle Sam, Sara, and I—held onto her. He began to lose his temper. He cursed and gave Uncle Sam a hard kick. Uncle Sam let out a cry but didn't move. A few heads turned towards us.

Suddenly, a whistle. The train jerked. The man looked at Helka, spit in anger and jumped off the roof. I kept my eyes on him until the train picked up speed.

* * *

As on the first frightening trip to Germany, in November 1942, the train passed through monotonous landscape. It moved at a good pace as we talked about Regensburg. Uncle Sam and Sara had many questions about Regensburg's location, size, and how it felt to live among the Germans. I was about to give them answers when I noticed the train slowing down. The con-ductor returned, handing back everyone's documents. "We are approaching the Polish/German border," he told us. "Have your luggage and documents ready." He repeated this several times as he made his way through the train.

"Great. We're making progress," I said.

When we worked our way off the roof and into the long line of pas-sengers, it felt good to touch the ground again. Where the train had stopped seemed to be in the middle of nowhere. No station. No town. We waited a long time before the line began to move. The small building we finally reached had not been well kept up. In an open hallway, a few long tables took up most of the space. Russian military men sat behind the tables and carefully checked the documents and suitcases of every passenger. We made slow progress. Laughing and shouting Russians could be heard in the back of the building. Finally, our turns came. A tired-looking, stocky young man hardly bothered to check our suitcases. He looked at Helka's papers and gave them back to her. Uncle Sam, Sara, and I came next. At first, he looked rather quickly at our documents and was about to give them back to us, when suddenly he stopped. He studied the photos and looked at each of us in a strange way. Without a word he got up and left. When we had waited some time, I began to worry. Most everybody had been cleared. I feared we would be the only ones left.

Over half an hour later, he came back and waved at us to follow him. He motioned for Helka to stay, saying something in Russian. He did not answer any of our questions, asked in Polish and German. He took Uncle Sam, Sara, and me down to the basement. A terrible place. Dim, damp and messy, the dirt floor was covered with torn pieces of paper, chicken feathers that flew into the air with the slightest motion, and empty vodka bottles.

He led Uncle Sam into one room, showed Sara and me into another one. The rooms (there were three or four of them) had the same dirt floor, no furniture and no doors. A wide gap connected each room with the hallway. The man again said something in Russian and left. Sara and I were petrified.

"Why did they put us here? What did we do wrong?" we asked each other.

Uncle Sam left his cell and came to be with us. In a voice he tried to control, he said, "It's obviously a mix-up. It doesn't make any sense. They will let us out any minute."

The minutes turned into hours, and soon darkness fell. The loud laughter of the men upstairs moved closer. Two young soldiers came wobbling down the steps. With their windblown hair and unbuttoned uniforms, they sang and waved the half-empty vodka bottles. They looked at Sara and me, and began to walk towards us. One of them, focused on me, took a few steps and came closer and closer. I felt trapped but didn't want to scream. With my arms crossed, I stared at him and moved slowly back.

To my surprise, our slightly built, elderly uncle stepped between the drunk soldiers and us. With a stern look, in Russian I could barely understand, he said something. The two of them were taken aback. They glanced at each other and looked at Sara and me. The older blond man threw his cigarette on the bare floor, stepped on it, twisting his foot back and forth. He scratched his head and gazed through the tiny window. Suddenly he swung around and motioned to the other one. Their heavy steps going up the stairs resonated throughout the basement.

The night passed fitfully. Early in the morning, a tall, imposing looking young lieutenant, with several medals on his uniform, came down. He held the documents and asked for our names. Uncle Sam, encouraged by his success with the soldiers the night before, answered the lieutenant's questions. He knew some Russian from growing up under their occupation. But then, something went wrong. The officer's face grew red, his smallpox scars more prominent. He accused us of trying to destroy our documents. He suspected espionage.

"Me a spy?" Uncle Sam cried out. "I've been Communist all my life."

"Prove it. Where is your red card?"

"Red card? I was just liberated from a concentration camp. I have no papers from before the war."

After an uneasy silence, Uncle Sam asked: "Could I speak to the commandant?"

"I am the commandant" came the short answer.

"Could I see your superior?"

"I have none."

The man seemed to savor his words. He smiled to himself and left. His strong steps and the loud whistle terrified us.

We were finished. The three of us were accused of spying on the Soviet Union. I had heard about the Soviet justice system. They shot first, asked questions later. After surviving Hitler and the allied bombs, we might just face a quick execution right there in the middle of nowhere in a filthy old building or live to take a long trip to Siberia. Our despair grew.

Suddenly I recalled the friendly, Russian conductor collecting our papers on the train. He had put Helka's papers in a large black bag. But the bag was too full for our documents, and he stuffed them into his pocket. Helka's papers remained smooth, ours got wrinkled. We had to act right away. But I had no idea where the young conductor was then or how we could reach him. Because Helka was not allowed to visit us, we gave her the news through the small basement window. It took her some time to find him.

"You have to help me," she pleaded with him. "Please . . . help me. My sister, cousin, and uncle are under arrest. Their documents looked wrinkled, and the commandant accused them of spying. Remember when you took them from us on the train? You put my papers in the large bag and theirs in your pocket because you ran out of space."

His smile vanished as he looked at her. He shoved his cap and pulled on his ear. "Oh, yes, I do remember. There was you, two other girls, and an older man. Arrested? How stupid! Just wait here," and he disappeared.

It seemed like an eternity before he came back. He held the documents in his hand.

After they let us go and we turned the corner, we didn't walk—we ran—to the train station.

33

The rest of the trip passed uneventful. In Regensburg, Uncle Sam and Sara loved everything about the villa: the quiet neighborhood, the sun-filled rooms, the balcony overlooking the small, well-kept garden, and especially the indoor bathroom. No comparison with the run-down apartment in Piotrkow. The four of us became a family. It felt good to have an older person with us. Since our parents were gone, Uncle Sam had to fill the void. He had to replace Sara's mother, and the aunts and uncles we once had.

During our absence, the number of survivors who had settled in Regensburg had grown. So had the new Jewish Committee taking care of their needs. They became an efficient organization that functioned well.

New survivors still trickled into the city. Marysia was one of them. I don't remember when and how we met, but she recognized Helka and me right away and cried out: "I know you. You're the two sisters from Neustadt/ Orla who ran away. It's you. I am sure it's you."

"How do you know?" I asked.

"I was in the *Lager* long before you came. I remember that one day my best friend, the Polish girl Ala, pointed at the two of you and whispered: 'Those two are Jews. What are they doing here? Let's send them back to the ghetto where they belong.'

"'Jews? It's impossible. How would they have gotten here?' I replied.

"'Don't be naive, Marysia,' said my friend. 'They found a way and are trying to fool us. I can spot any of them right away.'

"And I will never forget the Friday when you ran away. That evening somebody noticed your empty bunk beds, and a storm broke loose. At first only a few paid attention, but soon many of them shouted: 'The two sisters who ran away are Jews, and we have more of them here. We need the Gestapo.'

"And the Gestapo came. It took them a few weeks, but when they came, they arrested all of us."

Of the many girls Marysia mentioned, I remembered only Halinka and Zosia, the two stunning friends from Warsaw.

They moved the arrested Jewish girls to a prison in a larger city. The Gestapo interrogated one at a time. While Marysia waited her turn, a young Polish man in an adjoining cell (a member of the underground movement back home) struck up a conversation with her. After learning her name and what town she was from, he exclaimed, "You are Marysia? I can't believe it. I knew your older sister. I remember you, too. Let's meet during the break."

She was petrified. Her false papers belonged to her friend, the real Marysia, and this man, behind the wall, knew that young woman. She was sure that this would be the end. When they met in the prison courtyard, he was stunned. "You're not Marysia. I know you. You lived on Nowa Street. Felicia, right? Don't worry. I'll help you."

He became her witness. He testified that she was from his hometown, he knew her, and their families belonged to the same church. The Gestapo released her.

Marysia wasn't sure whether anyone else of the arrested young women made it. For the rest of them, Auschwitz was the final destination.

Marysia became our frequent guest and, during one of her visits, met Felix. Felix, our cousin from Piotrkow, had lost his wife and a baby during the ghetto liquidation. He had worked with our father and Natek at the Bugaj forced labor camp. Felix and Marysia fell in love and got married.

* * *

One late afternoon, a young man, of slight build and with a winter coat too long for him, came to see us. I couldn't tell who he was, but Helka knew right away: "It's Paul, our cousin from Lukow. Our mother and his father were siblings."

Paul's story followed in similar fashion to the stories of other young men from Eastern Poland. He had escaped to the Soviet Union, where they sent him from one labor camp to another. Siberia was the worst. After the war, when he returned home, he found no one. His family had consisted of his parents, four brothers, and two sisters—a family of nine. Besides himself, only Pola, his younger sister, had survived and had been sent to London as a war orphan.

Pola, only twelve when the war broke out, managed on her own to obtain false Polish papers. (The details of her ordeal, however, are lost as she has been unable to talk about what happened to her.)

Paul didn't remain long at the villa. He moved to Munich to enroll in dental school.

* * *

Quite unexpectedly a letter arrived from Richard. Actually from Richard and his mother to Uncle Sam and Sara. The two families knew each other in the ghetto and in the camps.

I felt thrilled that he had survived and that I would get to see him. When he and his mother came to visit, his mother, Uncle Sam, and Sara talked about the camps and the people who had survived and those who had not—the common topic. Uncle Sam had lost his wife and a daughter (Hanka) and she her youngest son. Richard had been with him in the concentration camp but couldn't save him. He wasn't able to talk about it.

Ever since I had escaped from Piotrkow, even though I didn't know what had happened to him, I had a premonition that Richard would live.

When I finally saw him, he hadn't change much. Maybe his face looked paler and his body skinny. His reddish hair seemed thinner, but his smile remained the same.

Richard vaguely remembered me. In the Piotrkow ghetto, he had had many friends and a girlfriend, but I liked him then and I still did. I delighted in being in the same room with him talking about our families and friends. Most of them had not survived. He appeared stunned when he heard my war story. "You must have been in constant fear. Where did you get the courage?"

I could have talked to him for hours.

As we talked, I had a new surprise. Richard also planned to go to medical school. It was the fall of 1945, most of the German universities remained closed, except in Heidelberg, a city untouched by the war. We

160

decided not to waste time and applied to the old, famous, medical school there. The train rides and the enrolling process gave us a lot of time together.

Shortly afterwards UNRRA (United Nations Relief and Rehabilitation Administration) University in Munich opened. Since it was closer to Regensburg, where Helka, Uncle Sam and Sara lived, I registered there. So did Richard.

The school, located in the *Deutsches* (German) Museum in the center of town, had a few rooms and a handful of teachers, all foreigners with different accents. We, the students, were happy to have any school. The only professor I still remember was a tall, unassuming Ukrainian who taught physics. An older man, he gave good lectures and seemed easily accessible. As I recall, the students were Poles, Ukrainians, Latvians, Lithuanians, and Jews. Each nationality clung to their people. All my friends were Jews.

After the long, horrible interlude, I finally had returned to what I loved most and had waited for so long—the classrooms, lectures, professors, and students. And Richard. I even lived in a much larger town. Munich, once a beautiful city, in large part lay in ruins. Piles of bricks and charred wooden beams blocked streets and sidewalks. Grotesque remnants of the old, elegant buildings stared back at onlookers. Getting around proved quite a challenge. Richard and I had to walk on top of and around those high piles of rubble, which rain made even more treacherous. I didn't mind.

And that's how it started. We attended classes, made new friends and studied together. Many hours together. Richard, always bright, learned fast,

Richard and Sabina in Frankfurt. Spring 1947.   Richard's mother and Sabina. Spring 1947.

Me, visiting Richard in Frankfurt. Spring 1947

Richard. Spring 1947

Helka, Joseph, Sabina, and Richard. Munich, winter 1945-1946.

and the other students liked him. He took school seriously, and it became obvious that, with his abilities and compassion, he would make an excellent doctor.

After the Frankfurt Medical School reopened, he decided to transfer there to be with his mother.

"Oh, Rysiek (diminutive name), tell the truth," I teased him. "You want to look for a pretty girl."

"Of course . . . come here," and he pulled me close. There were many letters, many visits. Anticipation between visits became misery.

And this went on for over a year. I could tell his mother liked me, too. Everything seemed to be going the way I hoped.

Then one day a telegram came from Frankfurt: with a date and details of Richard's . . . funeral. Two days before, on a hot June day, he and his friends went swimming in the river, as a break while studying for the exams. Before he returned to his books, Richard took one last dive . . . in a spot too shallow for diving. He broke a vertebra in his neck, and for a while he remained unnoticed under the water. Paralyzed, he lived but a few hours.

Unnoticed under the water? If I had been there, he wouldn't have been unnoticed. And I had just visited. He had asked me to stay longer, and I hadn't. I should have. I wouldn't have let him jump.

I took the train to Frankfurt (my worst trip ever). Like a short in a movie theater, images swam before my eyes: the river, his friends, and Richard . . . jumping in. The river, his friends, and Richard . . . jumping in. Over and over in front of my eyes . . . even with my closed eyes.

His body lay in a remote part of the hospital. The large room had steel cabinets, large sinks, and a

Richard's funeral. June 1947.

cement floor. Maybe a pathology lab or a morgue. I couldn't tell. Richard lay motionless on a long, wooden table. His eyes closed, his smile gone. He felt cold when I bent down and kissed him. The stubs of his beard and the fingernails seemed long, having grown after death. Someone cut off a lock of his hair and gave it to me, his coarse, reddish hair. I did not stay long. I couldn't.

The funeral was small, the people strangers. His brother, like the other men, wore a wide-rimmed hat and prayed silently. His mother's ghost-white face said it all. Shock, disbelief, pain. It looks like a powerful, tragic painting. I still have the photo. She needed my support as she stood on the edge of the grave.

My body shivered. I moved in a daze. I wanted so badly to believe it was only a dream, a bad dream. Not real. It couldn't have been.

* * *

When I returned to Munich, everything annoyed me. Nothing had changed. The city bustled with the same streetcar clatter and the same talk and laughter of the people on the sidewalks. The classes, the professors, even my friends continued as before. I couldn't stand it. Especially my male friends. My mind would focus on one of them at a time. They were still there, and their lives continued. Richard was the one in the ground, the deep, dark ground of the Jewish Cemetery in Frankfurt. Why had it happened to him?

For a long time, everything reminded me of Richard: the shores of the Isar River, the park, and our favorite small restaurant. "Your eyes are still in the wet place," was Helka's frequent remark.

I kept in touch with Richard's mother after that tragic June day of 1947. I wrote to her, visited her. But after she left Germany, our contact gradually came to an end.

I continued my studies, and the resentment, anger, and pain slowly began to ease.

34

Helka, Uncle Sam, and Sara remained in Regensburg. They served on the Jewish Committee, which looked after the survivors. Uncle Sam became a committee member, my sister and Sara worked in the office. They supported themselves and continued to live together in the villa. Regensburg became home to them and a home base for me. A two-hour train ride from Munich brought me back frequently.

Munich and medical school, made possible by free tuition and a small stipend from the American Jewish Organization, became my world, a damaged world without Richard. The scarce coal and rationed electricity left my room dark and cold a good part of the time. With streetcars unpredictable, I did a lot of walking in the wet snow, getting frostbite on my toes. I watched German women scramble from one empty grocery to another. That, at least, didn't last very long. The American Marshall Plan filled the stores with shipments of food and prevented wide-spread hunger—not like under the German occupation in my hometown. Hunger in our ghetto had left many adults and children dead and dying in the streets.

Because of intense allied bombings during the war, housing shortages grew critical for the newly arriving students. It was almost impossible to find a room to sublet. The Housing Office found families with extra space and ordered them to take in additional people.

That's why, when I moved from Regensburg to Munich and arrived at the apartment on Zumpe Strasse with the official piece of paper, I didn't receive a friendly reception. The middle-aged, shy woman who opened the door looked stunned and frightened. She kept saying *"Jawohl, Fraulein"* ("Yes, miss"), without looking at me. Her husband remained in a POW camp somewhere in Russia, and she had been ordered to sublet one of her rooms. She kept the large room and gave me the small one. I was to share the kitchen, but I didn't feel welcome and used a small electric hot plate in my room instead. Her teenage son slept in the kitchen next to the bathroom. As a result, I never used the bathroom at night and only seldom during the day. I walked to the public toilets several blocks away.

The apartment was on the third floor (no elevators). My room had a single bed, a table, a wash bowl with a water pitcher, and an old wardrobe. A lot of light came through the large window, and I liked it there.

I was able to help some of the newly arrived students, who knew no German, in the Housing Office. The Jewish students, who constantly streamed in, formed a pitiful group. They had survived Hitler's persecutions as partisans, in hiding, on false papers, in Russia, and in the concentration camps. The concentration camp inmates arrived in the worst shape. Many of them, the only survivors of large families, had been physically and emotionally damaged. The emotional recovery took far longer and was more difficult. Even though, unlike so many others, I found myself able to talk about the war, the fear, nightmares, and grief remained with me.

Visiting the few friends who had living parents seemed unreal to me. Mothers' and fathers' faces glowed when they looked at their sons and daughters. They were there to nourish, give advice and take pride in them. Their homes were warm and full of love.

My room felt cold and bare. Both my parents gone, and no grave to visit.

* * *

Slowly the war memories began to give way to current needs and interests. Luckily, in spite of the physical and emotional harm, minds functioned well. We did not brood all the time. We had formed a Jewish Student Union, which represented us and was able to deal effectively with various German officials. When Munich University reopened, my friends and I transferred from the UNRRA. A Jewish Student Committee screened, gave exams, and if needed, offered prep courses to the applying students.

The Student Union was centrally located and easy to find, either on foot or by streetcar. It occupied space in a large building. With bare walls, a few desks, tables, and chairs—used furniture—it still seemed great to us. We picked up the food rations there, as well as used clothes and shoes from America. I loved bringing home the goodies. The food packages posed mysteries. I had no problems with the sardines, canned meat, and cocoa, but when I opened a can of tuna, peanut butter, or condensed milk, I was at a loss. I have never seen, let alone, eaten any of those foods. I would cautiously stick my finger into something new and taste it. A surprise—it was good, especially the sweet milk and the peanut butter.

I had more difficulty with the donated clothes and shoes, the shoes especially. I still have the calluses an elegant pair of black pumps left on my feet. One day I was forced to take them off in the middle of a busy street and walk barefoot for a long distance. I had an easier time finding the right clothes. I remember a warm, stylish, winter coat a seamstress made for me from a dyed army blanket. I loved it and wore it for a long time.

The union also provided various speakers. Guest speakers delivered the scientific or political topics while our own students liked to vent their feelings on many subjects. The elections of committee members were always lively. But the most popular gatherings—the informal ones. We spent considerable time just hanging out, getting to know each other. Lifelong friendships formed. I still keep in touch with my best friends from Munich—Marion, who lives in Israel, and Susie, in Australia. (They both practiced medicine and are now retired grandmothers like myself.)

The American Joint Organization also sponsored the dining hall. We all liked the *Bursa*, where, once a day in the early afternoon, a hot meal was available. The *Bursa*, located near the Student Union, occupied an open storefront near a busy intersection. Sparsely furnished and not too well kept up, it was packed most of the time. The food was okay. I could smell the beef stew, the cabbage-borscht, or the chicken soup (usually watery) before I entered the dining hall. The company, though, had as much value as the food.

"How was your physiology exam?" Sophie would call to me from across the hall. "Mine is next week, and I don't know if I am ready."

"Oh, come on, you always get A's," I said as we walked out together.

Helka and Sabina with cousins Paul and Pola, 1948, in Munich near the *Bursa* dining hall.

Many serious relationships, which often led to marriages, sprang up among our friends. One day, in the slow-moving line to the kitchen window, I overheard a young man ask Lida, one of my friends. "Where were you last night? I stopped to see you," but before she could answer, the line moved on, and I didn't hear the rest. A short time later, this caring young man found out he had lost Lida to a clever but unreliable guy.

* * *

Occasionally, the Joint Organization would sponsor a trip to the nearby Alps for the Jewish students. It instantly brought memories of Richard and me in the mountains. As a poor skier, I had often managed to have one of my skies stuck in the snow. He would laugh and laugh and take his time getting me up. This trip occurred in the summer, without him.

Clear lakes reflecting blue skies, small wooden houses hugging the tall mountains, and the snow-covered peaks—unforgettable. Berchtesgaden, a beautiful resort, where Hitler often stayed, became one of my favorites. After exams, a group of twenty or thirty students would meet early at the Munich railroad station, board a train and travel together. Even the train ride was fun.

We would stay in the most elegant hotels, the ones off limits to anyone but the Gestapo and the highest ranking German military just a short time before. At first, it felt spooky to be in those rooms. But we soon ignored the feeling, even liked the idea. If they only knew who enjoyed them. We had a great time. We threw parties for the slightest reason, or for no reason at all, talked about the past and the future and took long walks. None of us would have dared to dream about vacations only a short time before.

One time, a small group of four young men and three women, me among them, decided to take a short hike. As we walked, the view become breathtaking. The blue-green lakes with their glistening, pristine water nestled between the majestic mountains. The thick forest at the bottom would gradually turn into bushes, sparse greens, then naked walls. The year-round snow on the high peaks seemed to touch the sky. I had never seen snow in the summer. When it began to get dark, we hated to leave. We kept going higher and higher. Finally, we had to stop. We found a small hostel and spent the night there.

Watzman adventure in the Alps. Lida, Sabina, Natek, Susie, Emek, and others.

The next morning, impressed with our achievement, we continued to climb. We had already passed the green part of the mountain and were struggling with the huge boulders. By the afternoon, I was getting short of breath. I didn't realize this was normal at those heights, and had a hard time keeping up. It was scary to look down. Exhausted and frightened, we reached the peak of the Watzman, one of the highest mountains in the German Alps. After feasting our eyes on the unbelievable beauty around us, we took a short rest. To leave proof of our conquest, we tied a colorful handkerchief to a small wooden stick and planted it on the peak of the Watzman.

Going down proved less strenuous but treacherous, easier to slip and fall. As I looked around, I suddenly realized how high we had climbed. I only hoped to make it back to the paved streets of Berchtesgaden.

When we returned to the hotel, dead tired but proud, none of our friends believed our story. "We were really foolish," said Natek. (Same name as my brother.)

"And lucky," added Emek.

Our two leaders had little experience, but we had followed them with enthusiasm. They were right. We had no professional guide, no proper shoes, no equipment, and I don't think any of us had ever climbed a mountain like the Watzman. We were young, daring and perhaps had to catch up after years of fear and constraint.

* * *

The museums and theaters of Munich gave me another surprise. I thrilled to be able to see an art exhibit, a play, or an opera. I still remember the tears I shed for the poor Madame Butterfly. *Kleine Komedie* (the Small Comedy Theater) was my second favorite place. The performances held to a high artistic level, and student tickets stayed extremely reasonable. We gladly stood in the rush lines.

It felt great to be alive, to be free, to have the chance to catch up on my education and make plans for the future. My cousin Hanka came to mind. My dearest Hanka, small in body, big in mind and goals. Determined and focused. Because of the war, she never achieved the education she desired, or helped to build the Jewish State. She went to fight the Germans. She never came back. Hanka died, and I lived. I found it difficult to reconcile this.

35

While well into the medical school routine, I would feel the old trepidations coming back. I wondered why I still lived in Germany and studied at a German university. After what had happened in the war, I felt that I should have been hoping, as soon as possible, to

Munich group. Sophie sits next to me (back row).

leave the country and the people who had brought so much evil into the world. Reality, of course, had changed my plans. Though the Germans had lost the war, they still had their families and their country. The Jews had won, in a sense, but most of us had no families, no homes, and no country. To have remained in Poland with loss all around me would have been too painful.

Because I knew no French or English, my college choices in Europe slimmed. To emigrate, to Israel or America, without a medical degree would have ended my dream. I had little choice but to stay in Germany, in the American zone at the *Ludwig Maximilian Universitat-München*.

At first, I had a hard time leaving the UNRRA University. I was quite content there. Made up entirely of foreigners, we didn't share classes with German students, or listen to German professors. I feared entering the all-German institution. But since the UNRRA was academically inferior, and most of the students were leaving, I had no choice. The first few days, after I switched, proved quite difficult. After the war ended, I had kept a distance from the Germans and hoped to continue to do it. But suddenly I found myself right in their midst. The old, ivy-covered school buildings seemed threatening because of the bullet holes, the missing doors, and boarded-up windows. When I stood in line to register for classes, I had German students in front of me and German students behind me.

I found the crowded classrooms to be the worst part. It made me almost physically ill to look at row after row of young Germans. Especially the men, who, until recently, must have been German soldiers or even Gestapo. I didn't want to know where they had been during the war or what they had done to the Jews. I did not want to know, but I had to sit next to them.

To be able to sit next to each other, my Jewish friends and I took turns arriving quite early in the morning and reserving several seats. Some brought folding chairs, and many remained standing throughout the lectures. The classrooms were so crowded that, on hot summer days (air conditioning didn't exist), someone always fainted. A few times, I had to leave the classroom.

Another problem—the lack of textbooks. We had to rely on the notes we took during a lecture. I found it impossible to keep up with a professor and write down everything he said. I remember only one person able to do it—Fira, the sister of my best friend, Susie. Ambidextrous, she kept switching her pen from one hand to the other. She had better, more complete notes. We all hoped to borrow them.

A solution to the problem soon appeared. A young, resourceful assistant professor offered—at a premium price—private tutoring classes and included typed material. A loan from Helka, by now engaged to Ben, got me into a couple of them. I haven't repaid her yet.

The medical school buildings had been damaged in the war, and the classrooms remained crowded, but the professors gave good lectures. If they only lasted. The anatomy professor, Professor von Lanz, a tall, handsome, aristocratic-looking man of quick stride and command, had good classes and became quite popular. One day as he wrote on the blackboard, explaining in great detail the location and function of the shoulder and back muscles, he suddenly stopped and called for someone. The elderly janitor, whom I had passed in the hallways many times, appeared in front of the students . . . stark naked. The professor began nonchalantly marking in red pencil the muscles on his body. He had him raise and lower his arms, straighten and relax his back. I felt my face getting hot. I didn't want to look. The only thing I learned that day was that the elderly, stooped janitor obeyed orders well.

Another morning when the crowded classroom expected Herr Professor von Lanz to march in confidently, a young, rather meek, assistant professor came in. He mumbled some explanation for his presence and began the lecture about the muscles and ligaments of the leg. He did not ask for the janitor.

Soon, a whispered explanation. Professor von Lanz had been arrested for his Nazi activities during the war. I never saw him again.

Because of the extensive damage to the medical school, we couldn't use the labs and became accustomed to a lot of theory and little practice. The pathology lab became one of the few exceptions. I still remember my first class. As I entered the large room, a strong smell of formaldehyde hit my nostrils. Sealed glass bottles with strange particles floating in the murky fluids filled the counters and shelves. Parts of bloody organs lay around the sinks and a few microscopes stood idle on a table next to the window.

After a short wait, the professor, a pleasant young woman in her thirties, walked in. "I am going to demonstrate an autopsy. You can ask any questions you might have, but please remember, only a few days ago, the cadavers were live people like any of us. They deserve respect. Now, please move closer to the table."

A protruding long object lay covered with a white sheet. When she threw back the sheet, a naked body, that of a well-built, middle-aged man faced me. He hardly looked dead. The professor felt her way at the bottom of the man's (I couldn't call him a cadaver) neck and placed her two fingers in the small indentation above the sternum. With, what seemed to me, lightning speed, she dragged the glistening steel scalpel all the way down to his pubic hair . . . a long gap opened. Cut tissue and droplets of blood came to the surface.

Live Jews in concentration camps had been cut for "medical experiments." Thoughts of this came to mind. I felt faint and moved away.

As time went by and I became accustomed to the German students next to me, I was in for a new surprise. I had naively assumed that Hitler's anti-Semitism was fading. During a psychiatry class, the elderly, soft-spoken professor discussed, I think, schizophrenia. He talked about the symptoms, diagnosis, and the treatment of the disease. As usual, he sent for a patient to demonstrate the symptoms. A shy woman, of indeterminant age, was brought in. Of slight build, she had graying hair and wore a drab, wrinkled dress. She faced the professor, but with her eyes cast down. At first she answered his questions correctly, but then out of the blue, her eyes lit up, her face turned red, and, staring into the unknown, she shouted: "The Jews are buying up our best chickens!" Just as quickly, it ended. Her eyes fell, and her face lost its expression.

The students roared. They stamped their feet, clapped and whistled. This went on for quite some time, long after the woman fell silent again. I was shocked and hurt. If this was the new, democratic Germany, then nothing had changed.

A German student, who sat in front of us, turned around, and, obviously upset, kept repeating: "Don't pay attention to those idiots. I am sorry. I am very sorry."

Meanwhile, I attended classes, prepared for and took many exams. All exams in the medical school in Munich, at that time, were oral. Two or three students would meet with the professor and answer his questions. I don't remember if they gave us the grades right away, but we knew whether we had passed or failed. Hardly any of us studied alone. My friend Marion, who lived one flight below me, was my partner for several subjects, and Ben and Moniek for the rest. This system worked well. We took turns reading aloud the text, asking questions and giving the answers. We felt this made the long, tedious hours go faster. But, I see now, it was mainly the need to have friends near by. Being alone would let the scary, sad thoughts come back.

36

From 1945 until 1950, much happened. Hitler had lost the war. The friendship between the United States and Soviet Union, allies at the end of the war, turned sour, initiating the Cold War, and the Iron Curtain fell across Europe. Israel became an independent Jewish State, and Western Europe mended its wounds.

Sabina and a close friend, Marion, in Munich. Marion later moved to Israel.

Sabina and Susie. Munich, 1946. My dress was made from window drapes. Susie later moved to Australia.

Sabina (right) in Munich. The winter coat had been made from a United States army blanket.

I spent the five years in Munich productively and happily, except for Richard's tragic death and my parents' absence. I received my medical degree, made many friends, some for life, had a few romances and met Ruben.

Ruben and I met at the graduation party he and his roommate gave after receiving their electrical engineering degrees. I still chuckle when I think about it. As I danced with Romek, the friend with whom I had come, I noticed Ruben, of muscular build and confident manner. Happy and loud, he beamed, his brown eyes twinkled, and the curly hair tangled. Dancing, he inadvertently bumped into me. When I made a remark, he said: "I don't know you. You don't know me. This is my place, and I can do what I want." He liked to speak his mind.

Shortly afterwards Ruben joined the group of friends that included Romek and me. Since Romek faced exams for his Ph.D. in chemistry and was occasionally absent, Ruben began to come up with new, better plans, better for the two of us. We went to the movies, to his favorite neighborhood restaurant and took long walks.

Before I knew it, we dropped the rest of the group. Ruben and I began meeting more and more often and tried to avoid Romek. Ruben respected him and felt guilty about the situation. Even though Romek was gentle and caring, his cold, moist hands lost out to Ruben's warm, strong ones. The break up was painful for Romek and quite uncomfortable for me.

* * *

Ruben, from eastern Poland, had a completely different war story. At first he refused to talk about it. Then, one cozy evening in his sublet room, unexpectedly he began to talk about what he had experienced. "I had escaped to the Soviet Union in June of 1941, when Hitler broke the pact with Stalin and attacked eastern Poland—our part of Poland. This came as a complete surprise to the Soviet Union and a tragic surprise to us, the local Jews. We knew about the Nazi atrocities, and, had we had any warning, many could have escaped and survived. But there was no

Ruben (top) before leaving for the United States, 1949. Bottom, Ruben in Munich, 1948.

177

warning. It was summer, schools were out, and my family was scattered in different towns visiting relatives.

"I remember too vividly what happened. In the middle of the day, I was walking down the empty street of Dubno, my hometown. The Germans had bombed the city; the air raid alarm had just ended. Two friends passed me by. 'What are you doing here, walking so slowly?' one asked. 'Don't you know the Germans are coming?'

"'Yes, I heard it, but they are far away,' I said.

"'Far away? They're at the outskirts of town. We're going east. You can join us if you want to.'

"'Going east right away? Yes, I think I would like to go with you. But I have to talk to my parents first.'

"'Talk to your parents? The Germans are not after them. It's us, the young men who are in danger. You can write to them.' And they continued their brisk walk. I stopped. To leave, without talking to Mom and Dad? I hesitated for a second and began to walk home. But the empty streets felt eerie, and the two young men were fading in the distance. I turned around, ran and caught up with them.

"I spent the next four years in Russia, and it wasn't easy." He wouldn't say more. "After the war ended, I came back and found no one.

"My parents, my younger sister, Batia, and my little brother, Isaiah, . . . were all killed by the Germans." His voice began to break. "I don't even know when or how it happened. Uncle Jack and Uncle Leon, my mother's brothers with whom I had grown up, and two male cousins are the only ones left of our large extended family."

* * *

As he walked me home, after the somber evening, he asked: "How is your new place. Is the lady any nicer?"

"No, I am not as lucky as you. I had to vacate the room on Zumpe Strasse when the lady's husband returned from the POW camp in Russia. She never wanted me anyway. Now the second one isn't any better."

"Oh, don't worry. Things might improve."

I had my doubts. My new landlady on Schneckelburger Strasse, right around the corner from where I used to live, didn't want me either, but she sure was different. Tall, older and with an aristocratic air about her, she had a long title and insisted that everyone use it when addressing her. Her husband, when alive, had been a doctor and a general. The long title went something like: "Frau Schultz, widow of a doctor, widow of a general and some other ranks." She was proud of her title, and no part of it could be left out. She made sure of it. She shared a large, elegant apartment with her daughter and a teenage granddaughter.

Frau Trauner, an older German woman (who gave me the recipe for her warm potato salad which I loved) and a young policeman occupied two other rooms. The policeman spoke politely but visibly avoided me. Necessity or guilt—I never found out. The landlady didn't like me and didn't like my guests. She kept track of everyone who came to visit. She made my friends uncomfortable, and they preferred to whistle for me from across the street. After a while, I recognized my friends by their whistles.

* * *

Even though I had many good friends, Ruben became special. He cared about me more and more. His analytical mind and deep insight produced advice and solution whenever needed. I could share with him any problem. In some way, maybe in many ways, he took my parents' place.

I could tell that Ruben, who lost his family, needed me as well. We met nearly every day.

37

Big events occurred in Regensburg. Helka married Ben, the only one left of his family, who had survived some of the worst concentration camps. Handsome, of dark complexion and mature for his age, he had learned to be tough, daring and self-reliant. After the war, at the age of twenty-two, he started his own business and became quite successful. All of this appealed to my sister. After their short courtship—Ben was quite persistent—they got married in March 1947. Since I didn't live in Regensburg, I had missed the intimate reports of their romance. The wedding took place in the villa, and Helka prepared the whole party herself. She was the cook, the hostess, and the bride. She prepared the festive Jewish dinner for a large group of guests, impressing everyone, including my friends from Munich.

The next big event was Natek's return from France. Not quite sixteen, a tall, good-looking boy, but shy and

Natek, arriving from France. Regensburg, 1947.

withdrawn, he arrived upset after someone on the train stole his small suitcase with all his possessions. For several years, he and Father had only had each other. They remained together in Buchenwald until Natek lost him in a death march two days before the liberation. He didn't know that Helka and I had survived and assumed himself to be the only one left. As a war orphan, they sent him to France to a boys' home near Paris.

Natek, as well as the other boys, whose education the Germans had cut off at early childhood, learned French and various trades. He didn't like making ladies' purses and preferred to climb high ladders to paint houses. (He said recently, "At that age, I was daring, loved the outdoors and the bike they let me ride to Paris. I hoped to be able to buy one myself.")

He remembered an American military rabbi arriving at the boys' home with a large book. It had a list of the survivors. Unfamiliar names. Then, shock. He saw Helka's and my name. He wanted to leave right away, but the supervisors objected. "Why go back to Germany? Your parents are dead. You better stay in France."

After we heard from him, we started making plans to bring him back, but he arrived on his own. Five years had elapsed since we had seen each other. Natek had been eleven at our separation. He needed time to feel comfortable with us again. Since I lived in Munich while at medical school, lived in a sublet room and attended classes most of the day, he settled with my sister, her husband Ben, and Uncle Sam.

Uncle Sam was happy when his daughter, Sara, met and married a survivor from Poland. They wed in Amberg, not too far from Regensburg, where her future husband lived. The wedding ceremony and the party were happy but subdued like all the others. And again one survivor married another one. After the war, the Jewish newly-weds and the rest of us felt a need to stay together.

Uncle Sam, Sara, and her husband, Ruben (two Rubens in one family), left Germany first, headed for Milwaukee, Wisconsin, where my uncle's sister had settled long before the war.

The next ones to emigrate were Helka, Ben, and Natek. In the summer of 1949, they left for Minneapolis, Minnesota, a completely unknown destination. They had requested Milwaukee, where Uncle Sam and Sara lived, but the city had already filled its quota of refugees. "We can place you in Minneapolis, a town close by," officials told them. The close by stretched to 400 miles, a whole night's ride on the Greyhound bus.

Ben and Helka with Natek behind them. Regensburg, 1948.

Sarah and husband, Ruben. Regensburg, 1949.

Sabina and Uncle Sam. Regensburg.

Next to Israel, America was the most desired destination for Jewish survivors. The European countries still struggled to recover from the war, Australia seemed too far, and Canada not too promising.

Ruben left in the fall of 1949 for Los Angeles to join his Uncle Jack, who had sent him the required papers. Only my cousin Paul and I remained in Germany to finish our studies.

I found parting from Ruben difficult. He couldn't postpone his departure, and I still had exams to pass. I remember spending hours with him at the railroad station. The train ran late, and he kept repeating: "If you don't waste any time, you could be done in a couple of months."

Suddenly the conductor blew the whistle, the train slowly picked up speed, and Ruben dissolved into the horizon. I missed him right away. I missed his wit and self-confidence. I wished his warm hands and smooth skin stayed with me.

About a week after he left, I thought I heard his whistle one evening. I didn't believe it could be his, and I ignored it. But when I heard it again, coming from across the street, I knew it was he. I ran down the steps like lightning. There he was with the meek smile on his face. "There was an unexpected delay, and instead of waiting in Bremen, I asked for permission to return to Munich. They gave me two days."

Natek, leaving for the United States in 1949 at age eighteen.

His room had been rented, and I didn't dare have him visit so late. We spent the night in the park. The whole nippy night. We walked for a while and sat on a bench, keeping warm and dozing. Chilled, we walked again to warm up, then dozed again. Thus we passed a long, wonderful night.

After the two days, I went with him to Bremen. Another delay gave us a few more days. I stayed with him until the big ship pulled away.

In Los Angeles, Ruben stayed at first with his uncle, then rented his own room and began to save money from his modest income. In the weak American economy, he couldn't get a job as an engineer. He took whatever he found. His letters came every day, sometimes more than one a day.

I hit the books, made progress and counted the weeks.

One day Ruben wrote that he wanted to buy me a sweater he saw in a store window. Many letters with questions and answers went back and forth. By the time we decided on the size, the color, and the details of the embroidery, the sweater had been sold.

Another excitement—his plan to come back to Munich. "Not for good," he wrote. "Just until you finish the exams. It's taking you so long." I was petrified because of the complicated and strict immigration laws. One wrong move, and we might end up in Germany forever. After many letters, he gave up the plan. I did my part and took one exam after another. And I moved one more time.

I had had enough of the Frau Witwe Schultz (Mrs., the widow of Dr. and General Schultz . . .). When a friend told me about an available room and nice landlords, I took it. The new landlords, Herr and Frau Stein, an older couple with no children, lived nearby on Brahms Strasse. My new room, on the main floor of a good-sized apartment building, proved spacious, bright and well-furnished. Both Herr and Frau Stein showed friendship right away. Herr Stein, an importer of tulip bulbs, used to travel to Holland. He talked about it a lot and loved to show me the catalogs of various tulips. Frau Stein, a grayish, stooped lady, was friendly and cheerful. She enjoyed seeing my friends, who sometimes stopped by unannounced. (Telephones were scarce.)

Ruben, whom she "knew" from the photo on my nightstand, intrigued her. He looked very masculine, with no shirt on his suntanned chest, high in the Alpine Mountains. She watched the mailman for his daily letters and placed them in my room in the most visible spot. She would greet me with an excited: "You have another letter from your *Liebing* (darling)." I must have brought excitement into her life. On cold days, she would surprise me by having the fire going in the tall, ceramic oven in my room. I shared some of the food I got at the Student Union with the nice couple. When I told my friends that they let me use their bathtub once a week, no one would believe me. Private bathtubs and showers remained rare and precious at that time. Most people used the public baths, a few of them elegant and expensive. When I left Munich, I gave Frau Stein my warm rabbit-skin jacket she had admired. I was sorry that I had lived with them less than a year.

All three rooms in which I had lived during the five years in Munich were located near the Prinz Regenten Platz, a nice part of town, with tree-lined streets, monuments . . . and the damaged Opera House. More than once I wished that the high- or low-pitched, rehearsing voice would stop repeating the same aria over and over. My window faced the back of the Opera House, and with it open, I could not escape the struggling voice. Eventually I had heard enough to be able to distinguish the frustrated voice at the beginning of the rehearsals from the self-assured one at the end.

* * *

The immigration process for thousands of displaced persons, the Jews among them, turned out to be long and tedious. I made many trips on the streetcar to the CIA (called CIC then) offices on the far outskirts of town. Because I wasn't familiar with the American holidays, I found closed doors several times. I had never heard of Memorial Day, the Fourth of July, Labor Day, or Thanksgiving. The only national, non-religious holiday I remembered observing back home was Veterans' Day. We all celebrated the end of the First World War on November 11, 1918 . . . meant to be the end of all wars.

The endless interrogations took a lot of time. The CIA men spoke German because none of us knew English. Various officers conducted the mostly one-on-one sessions. The officers varied, but the questions did not: "Are you now, or have you ever been a member, or a sympathizer, of the Communist Party. Do you believe in the ideology, or do you know any Communists?" With the Cold War, and McCarthy's reign in the United States, nothing seemed more important than pursuing real or imagined Communists.

Some of the interrogations became outright threatening and required witnesses to confirm our statements. My friends and I would witness for each other when needed. Fira (the ambidextrous friend with the best lecture notes) signed some papers for me, when the CIA officer asked what we were studying. We told him. He said, "Oh, you are smart girls. You'll be doctors. The two of you should go to Hollywood and treat the rich actors."

A few of my friends didn't pass the grilling interrogations and were denied entry to the United States.

The American military doctors conducted long physical exams and ordered blood tests, urine tests, and x-rays. Any health problem, especially tuberculosis or a venereal disease, would bring instant rejection. I remember a young mother crying out, "Oh, God, what do we do now? All three of us passed, but our four-year-old Jacob didn't." Anxiety ran high for all of us wishing to immigrate. I breathed easy after the mailman delivered the small letter with the official permit to enter the United States.

* * *

In June 1950, I received my medical diploma (one in German and one in Latin) and was ready to leave. Many friends had already emigrated, and others had been scheduled soon to follow. We had no graduation festivities.

I had waited a long time for this day. At age twenty-seven, I was leaving behind Europe with all the painful and all the good years of my life. The thought of a new country and a new language filled me with apprehension. But the fact that Ruben, Helka, Natek, and Ben had already made the transition reduced the fear. As I had meager possessions, the preparations didn't take long. Neither did the farewells, since so few of my family and friends remained.

Sabina leaving Munich for the United States. June 1950.

Sabina and Ruben in Regensburg, 1950.

AMERICA

38

Bremen-Hafen, a port on the North Sea, had a large transit place for the thousands of displaced persons leaving Germany. It must have been a military camp because it still had a wire fence and armed guards. Long rows of barracks housed the emigrants. I stayed there a week before I completed all the tests. Checking of the documents, the medical inspections, DDT powder in the clothes and hair, and the shots seemed to take forever. Finally, the *General Greeley*, a large, ragged ship, pulled into the port. During the war, this hard-working military vessel brought thousands of GIs to Europe. After the war, it served as a transport for refugees to America.

Each ship had its own destination. The Bremen-New York route delivered the DPs to the Midwest or the East Coast, while the Bremen-New Orleans passage took them to the South or the West Coast. For an unknown reason, our ship went to both places. First, we traveled to New Orleans and unloaded some of the passengers. Then we continued to New York.

The two- or three-day layover in New Orleans, which I expected to be fun, turned out to be miserable. June—hot and humid weather. On top of that, the required passes to go off the ship proved hard to get. I could only watch with envy the pulsating, throbbing city spread out in front of me. The blaring music and the loud laughter were enticing, yet unobtainable. The young people in the streets had a great time, while we had to remain on board and perspire on the sticky boat. To make matters worse, the unexpected detour stretched the voyage from several days to over two weeks. It postponed the reunion with Ruben and my family. Traveling alone made the time drag even more.

Because the ship had two destinations, in the beginning it carried more passengers—those for New Orleans as well as New York. People packed into the ship, filling every bunk and cot. Families could share the same space, what little they found, but single men and women slept in separate halls.

Marines of various ranks ran the ship. Women supervised the house-keeping and kitchen, while men saw to the navigation and a small hospital. The immigrant-passengers helped in cleaning the ship, cooking the food and taking care of the sick. I remember being assigned with a group of women to scrub the walls and the floor of a large stairway. When we finished the job, a strict and imposing female sailor checked our work, found many faults and had us redo it. A young Jewish DP man became a kitchen helper. He tried to win me over with special food.

Though the ship suffered from overcrowding, the three daily meals the ship provided, I found decent and plentiful. But the high sea and the strong waves took it back quickly. Profuse vomiting kept me away from the food lines; even the smell of the kitchen brought on nausea. Luckily some pills dispensed to me brought relief.

A few days into the trip, the captain of the ship asked all the medical doctors to come forward. I, a newly graduated MD with a lot of theory but little practice, found myself assigned to the night shift in the small hospital. At that point, I feared the patients more than they feared me. Fortunately, I didn't have to save any lives. When one night a mother brought a crying baby with a high temperature, I had to struggle hard with the wriggling patient to catch a glance at its tiny throat. I didn't impress the mother with my medical skills.

Finally, on a hot June day in 1950, *General Greeley* reached the port of New York. During my night duty, I could hear the intense activity. Mothers packed, and the fathers carried the family bundles and suitcases. The kids squirmed and jumped for joy. Everyone pushed and shoved in the long lines. At four in the morning, we began to disembark, leaving the cavernous ship behind. My sleepy eyes needed time to adjust to the first rays of the morning sun. My first morning in America.

When I stepped off the shaky plank of the boat, the first Americans I saw were members of the Daughters of the American Revolution. The ladies smiled, greeted every one of us and offered coffee and donuts. Their coffee tasted too strong, the donuts too sweet, and I couldn't understand a word they said. I had no idea how I would manage without English or how long it would take me to learn it. I had never experienced it before. In Poland language came on its own, and in Germany the four years of previous study helped a lot. It gave me a solid base on which to build. I had tried to learn English in Munich, but I had neither the time nor the money to study long enough. The few lessons from the private teacher didn't get me very far. Just the opposite, it made me realize how serious my problem was. I had never felt so helpless. I feared that, without English, my medical diploma would be useless. I was happy to be in America but scared and filled with doubts.

A shrill voice interrupted my thoughts. "Line up for the immigration and customs checks. Have your documents and luggage ready." Hundreds of DPs instantly formed a long line. The young, friendly man at the counter asked for my final destination, glanced at my papers and didn't bother with the suitcase. I could hear loud voices in many languages. A young woman from our ship waved and shouted to a group across the line. She spoke in Czech or Yugoslav. The new and not-so-new Americans waited for arriving relatives. I searched for Ruben's face. Finally, I found him squeezed into a corner.

He looked tired after the Los Angeles to New York trip. He had ridden a Greyhound bus three days to meet me. He stood next to Felix, my cousin from Piotrkow. As we got closer, Ruben and I stared at each other. Nine months of separation had finally ended. We shared a quick hug and kiss among the strangers. The rest would come later.

We spent about a week with Felix, his wife, Marysia, and their two children. After reminiscing again and again about Piotrkow, Regensburg, and Munich, we began to take in the sights of New York.

Besides the museums, the historical places, skyscrapers, and the famous Fifth Avenue, what overwhelmed me most—the heavy traffic, the crowds of rushing people, stores open in the middle of the night, and the forever-blinking neon lights. The ethnic and racial diversity took me by surprise. Before the American occupation, I had never seen anyone of color. New York formed a vibrant, exciting microcosm. Each ethnic neighborhood with its own language, culture, and religion reminded me of the small towns in Germany, Poland, and the Yiddish *shtetls* in Eastern Europe.

The train, which took twenty-four hours to get to Minneapolis, wasn't fully occupied, and we had a comfortable ride. I sat at the window and let my eyes glide over the hills, woods, rivers, and the open land.

I had seen such scenes many times in Europe. In the last few years, I had traveled a lot. Too much. On foot and on trains. There was always a need to run. Helka and I had escaped from the Piotrkow ghetto and went on foot to Radomsko to volunteer for work in Germany. It was the safer way. After they arrested us at the Neustadt railroad station, we went on foot to the next station.

The train rides weren't much better. Instead of pretending to be Poles, we had to pass as German girls. Fear was our steady companion, but we had no choice.

Travel after the war had no fear. Except the trip to Richard's funeral, trains took me to the mountains for vacation and to Bremen to leave Germany. The long, tedious ship journey brought me to America, and this train would take me to Minneapolis and to a new life.

39

I had not seen Helen (the American version of Helka), Nate (Natek became Nathan), and Ben for about a year. Ben and Nate had menial jobs because of language problems and worked all day. Helen, a new mother, had a cute ten-month-old baby girl. Little Dorothy was a good baby. She wasn't the best eater and woke up at least once during the night, but that gave me a chance to feed her and hold her until she fell asleep. "Helen, go back to bed," I would tell her. "You have a long day ahead of you. I love to do it."

Helen, a great housewife and a great mom, cooked, cleaned, washed, and even ironed the baby's cloth diapers. Ben and Helen rented the lower apartment in a duplex near a park. Helen easily communicated with the owners and most of her neighbors, Jewish immigrants from a generation before. Helen hardly needed English. The neighborhood, on the Northside—the north part of Minneapolis—with Plymouth Avenue the bustling main street, brought back memories of my childhood in Piotrkow before the war. Even though these streets were wider, with no cobblestones or crooked sidewalks, it felt familiar.

The deli restaurant caught my eye right away. I could smell the pastrami and corn beef. Crowded much of the time, the guests seemed loud and happy. The small grocery stores, the fish and meat markets, and the bakeries with the familiar rye bread and excellent pastries looked just like the ones I remembered. "Oh, Marvin, I see you didn't save a well-baked *hallah* (a Shabbath bread) for me. You know my husband doesn't like the saggy ones," complained a disappointed lady.

"Well, you're late. I didn't think you needed any. Tell Harold he'll get it next week. I will see you in the *shul* (the synagogue)."

Customers and storeowners knew each other well, and shopping was as much a social visit as a business transaction. It reminded me of Mother's shopping back home. She had been good with people. Anyone with whom she ever dealt had trusted and respected her. I missed her. I missed her presence, her wisdom, and her love.

Fridays in Minneapolis followed a frenzied pace, and the Saturdays relaxed. Just like back home. Whole families in their best clothes, walked (observant Jews do not drive on Shabbath) to the large and small synagogues close by. The synagogues back home had all been Orthodox, while in this neighborhood we had some Conservative ones, with fewer strict rules. The Reform, most liberal, synagogue, was located in the south part of town.

* * *

Ruben had found a job, not as an engineer (the market was still tight) but as a TV repairman, and the Jewish Family Service helped me to apply for the acceptance of my medical diploma. Luckily, the Munich Medical School was one of the approved foreign schools. It took several months of correspondence and meetings with the Minnesota Board of Medical Examiners before they granted approval. I remember facing a good-sized group of distinguished-looking medical doctors. They sat around a long table and asked questions. "When did the Munich University open up? How large were your classes? In what hospital will you do your internship?" Each man had a different question. In spite of my shaky English, I made it. The board members interviewed one person at a time. When I came out of the conference room, the waiting foreign doctors surrounded me. They wanted to know every detail of the interview.

The next challenge—passing the exams to receive a Minnesota Medical License. I knew I had a ways to go before I would be ready for that stage, and what I needed the most, English, would be invaluable in passing. I needed to study English intensely.

Ruben had excellent English, and he helped me with official visits and the correspondence. Not only had he been in the country nine months longer, he had studied the dictionary. With his great memory (his friends called him the walking encyclopedia), he would memorize a load of new words and use them.

I couldn't do that. For me conquering the English language was a hard nut to crack. Polish, my primary language had come on its own with no effort on my part. Since infancy my brain had soaked it up, and the language grew as I grew. We matured together. The rich vocabulary provided the fine nuances of my speech and writing. I loved it, but I had to leave it behind.

At nineteen, in the fall of 1942, when I escaped to Germany, I had difficulties with the new language. My pool of words had been limited and the pronunciation faulty. But the four years of German in high school had helped a lot. Knowledge of the grammar gave me a sound foundation on which to build, and, after a while, I read, spoke and wrote fluently.

I had to conquer English, my third language, but, unlike German, I had never been exposed to it. I didn't know a word of English, neither spoken nor written. Still, I needed it right away. Rather than brood or panic, I gathered my wits and tried self-education. Dictionary in hand, I attempted to read the newspapers. I could manage a few short lines under a picture of a movie star like Greta Garbo or Spencer Tracy.

I had better luck at the library. I asked for books written for adults but in simple language. To my great relief, the librarian understood. I still remember the very first book I read in English. It was about a mother of a Czech family, also new in this country, who cooked her children's favorite meals, making them from scratch. She spent a lot of time cooking. Pretty soon the word got out about her delicious food. Unexpected guests began to show up at dinnertime. The overwhelmed mother found a way out. She replaced the *schnitzel* and *pierogy* with hot dogs and canned beans. The guests stopped coming.

My progress seemed slow and frustrating. I hated my skeletal sentences of one or two words. I wasn't able to express myself in my usual eloquence, and my self-esteem suffered. I needed English to communicate and connect with people, especially when everything was new.

* * *

The situation improved when the Jewish Family Service found a woman willing to give me English lessons in her home. I don't remember her name, but she helped me a lot. I thought I was doing well . . . until the incident of the white blouse.

One day, the teacher invited Ruben and me to a dinner party at her home. I had never been to an American dinner party and wanted to be presentable. The black taffeta skirt I brought with me from Germany would be perfect if I found a new blouse.

I went downtown to Dayton's (now Marshall Field's) department store and, after trying on quite a few blouses, picked a white, glossy polyester. The skirt and blouse made a dressy outfit. Pleased with my selection, I went to the counter to pay for it. The young salesgirl finished helping the previous customer and turned towards me. She picked up the blouse from the counter and, while wrapping it, said with a pleasant smile, "Oh, you found a pretty one. Cash or charge?" She was about to hand me the package when she repeated, "Cash or charge?"

I had no idea what she meant. I had expected some small talk, and I waited patiently. But the "Cash or charge? Cash or charge?" I continued to wait. Her smile vanished, her voice grew louder. I knew I was irritating this nice, young woman. I felt the stares of the other customers. I struggled to find a way out. Suddenly, it hit me. "Money?" I whispered. She gave me a strange look. "Yes . . . money."

Instead of repeating the same words again and again, if the salesgirl would have tried different ones, I might have understood. Talking louder and louder may have helped a deaf person but not a newcomer to the country.

My problems didn't end yet. The dinner party of four couples was enjoyable, the food delicious, the company interesting, but my outfit—a fiasco. The other ladies wore casual, summer dresses.

In order to avoid similar situations because of my English, I found a simple solution. When approached with small talk, instead of struggling, I nodded, smiled and walked away. It worked for me many times.

Later on, I took an evening class at the university and did volunteer work at the Blood Bank, near Nicollet Avenue and Franklin. I knew I had to be among English-speaking people, rather than hide from them and use Polish with Helen or Yiddish with her neighbors.

40

The German in which I had been fluent for the past eight years became useless. I knew no one who spoke it. At times I felt as if a language war went on in my brain. When searching for a word, instead of English, a Polish or German word or expression would pop up. I never knew which language would take over or why. At first Ruben and I spoke to each other in Polish or German, but, after a while, without being aware of it, we began to use English more and more. It happened on its own. Later, when my vocabulary had improved but while I still spoke with a strong foreign accent, I found a pleasant surprise: general acceptance. Most people seemed curious about my native country and language.

"Oh, your accent's so cute. Where are you from?" became the common question.

Occasionally, I let them guess. They named exotic places. I had fun with this. Not at all as in Germany, where the minute an accent was detected, the person became an *Auslander* (a foreigner) at whom Germans looked down and didn't trust.

Being new in this country often made me feel like a small child overwhelmed with the world around me. So many things were different. The invigorating orange juice in the morning I found a novelty, and I liked to start the day with it. I never drank it in Europe. The dinner salad and raw vegetables became another great discovery. Back home we rarely ate salads, and vegeta-

197

bles were not only cooked but overcooked until they became limp and lost their vitamins. American fried chicken came as a delicious surprise. The chicken Mother used to serve, simmered on the stove for many hours to make chicken soup, had no taste compared to fried chicken. The quick and easy broiling seemed too good to be true. I didn't trust it at first and stayed away from it for a long time.

But I didn't find everything here better. The sliced white bread, a novelty at first, lost its delight as the bland taste and gooey consistence didn't measure up to the crusty Polish and German bread. For me, most of the pastries tasted too sweet and many other foods too salty. Fruits and vegetables back home, left until fully ripe because no one hurried to transport them to another part of the country, had better flavor. The price we paid for that was a lack of variety. We never had strawberries or tomatoes in the winter and ate only what was in season.

* * *

October 14, 1950, four months after I arrived in Minneapolis, Ruben and I married. In my sister's living room, the two of us stood under the *Huppah* (a silk canopy) as the elderly rabbi said the prayers. Ruben stepped on a wineglass, an old Jewish custom. The sound of the crushed glass brought applause and good-luck wishes. A homemade dinner followed the religious ceremony. Instead of our parents and other relatives, strangers came as guests.

In order to keep the wedding low key, especially financially, I decided not to buy a long white dress I would wear only once. I bought a light beige woolen dress and a small matching hat. The outfit quite pleased me. The dress fit well, and the hat gave a festive look. I wore the wedding dress all that fall and winter and left it in the closet in the spring. When the weather chilled, I took it out of the closet to wear again. But I couldn't. The dress practically dissolved in my hands, full of moth holes of various sizes.

Ruben also tried to keep the cost down. An expert photographer back in Munich, he decided to take and develop the pictures himself. He clicked away throughout our modest wedding festivities. A few days later, he gathered his equipment and went into the dark room. He opened the camera to take out the film . . . only to discover there was none. He had forgotten to put it in. We had no wedding pictures, no wedding dress. The only thing we had was our marriage. So far it has lasted fifty years.

* * *

I thought the apartment into which Ruben and I moved was the greatest. A small, one-bedroom upper duplex owned by an older couple, who lived downstairs with an unpleasant daughter, became our first home. I still remember her asking me what I did. When I told her I was a medical doctor, she said with great certainty: "You're a nurse. You just don't understand English." I let it be.

The small apartment needed considerable work. The two of us made improvements with great enthusiasm. We sanded the wooden floors, painted the walls and washed all the windows. The bathroom got a good scrubbing. The used furniture Helen's neighbors gave us filled the rooms and made me feel rich and important. I was in America, I was married, and we had our very own apartment. If only my parents could have seen us. Father would have been fifty-two. With his intellectual curiosity about the New World, I'm sure he would have read newspapers, and America had many newspapers.

I wrote about my new life to my friends in Munich, Israel, and anywhere else I could find them. And our life improved steadily. Ruben obtained a job as an engineer, and I continued to work in the Blood Bank as a volunteer. At first I only washed small petri dishes and glass bottles, but later on I drew blood for transfusions. None of the women with whom I worked made fun of my limited English or my accent.

One day a coworker remarked: "Why do you bring two sandwiches for lunch? Each of us has only one." I wasn't aware I did that and wondered why. As a child I had been a poor eater. Mother had to entice me with forbidden foods—unkosher sausages. Perhaps the years in the ghetto and food rationing that dwindled from scarce to starving had done it. The night with the sugar came to mind. But the war had ended and food became plentiful. I switched to one sandwich.

But I found myself different in other ways also. I tried to stay focused on important things in life, avoiding frivolities and excesses. Whenever friends or neighbors talked about their families, I went silent. My extended family had mostly perished. It hurt to think our children would never have grandparents. I would remain different.

When I began to cook for Ruben and me, I missed Mother again. She gladly would have taught me how to make all her favorite dishes. Instead of cookbooks, I turned to Helen, who remembered the recipes better and lived only a couple of blocks away. I also found running a household a novelty and felt the need for a schedule. I had always believed in plans and schedules. I decided to be efficient, do most of the house chores in one day, and enjoy the rest of the week. I couldn't understand why women bothered with it every day. Thursday seemed the best day. With most of the week over, having a clean house and good food for the weekend seemed a nice plan.

After work at the Blood Bank, which was in the south part of town, I would take the streetcar downtown to the Northern Market on Hennepin Avenue—one of the first supermarkets in town. I carried my groceries in paper bags to the streetcar. The ride home included a change to another streetcar, and when I got off I had several more blocks to walk. We had to manage without a car.

Once home, I would put away the groceries, prepare dinner and start to vacuum the rooms. After we finished eating, I did the dishes by hand. Ruben never volunteered to help. In addition to his work, he attended night school at the university, and, anyway, at that time, men managed to stay out of the kitchen.

Cooking chicken soup Mother's way required slow simmering for a long time. I would put it at low heat right after dinner and turn it off at bedtime. By the time I readied for bed, the chicken soup would be done and my weekly job finished. I felt proud of myself. I kept the routine for a while until that one Thursday evening when I got tired and lay down on the sofa. I had planned to take short nap but ended up sleeping through the night.

The next morning, I woke up to a pleasant aroma . . . the chicken soup still cooking on the stove. The meat fell apart into small, soggy chunks, naked bones floated around, and the very thick soup barely covered the bottom of the pot. Luckily I had not started a fire. I gave up that schedule.

41

Minneapolis began to feel more and more like home. Growing up, I had heard only of New York and Hollywood. After the war in Germany, I had read about Washington, D.C., Chicago, Los Angeles, and a few other cities, never Minneapolis. When I arrived, the city came as a big surprise. Large, especially by European standards, clean and attractive, I had never seen lakes so close to busy parts of town. The tree-lined, wide streets and the green parks gave the city a young, healthy look.

I was surprised at the name Twin Cites. If Minneapolis and St.Paul were twins, they must have been fraternal because they didn't look alike. St. Paul, smaller, older and the capital of the state, had a European flavor. Its beautiful old mansions, majestic Catholic churches, and narrow, hidden streets gave it a special charm but a slow growth.

Minneapolis, the younger, more modern city, vibrated with activity and grew at a fast pace. The large state university and several private colleges provided (and still do) the scientific basis for research and industry. Today Minneapolis is rich in culture. But it wasn't in 1950. When I left Munich and came here, I was shocked. Munich had its own State Opera, an Operetta House, and special theaters for classical, contemporary, folk and comedy plays. Some of the buildings remained damaged but the plays and the actors excellent. As a student with a reduced-price ticket, I had attended many great performances. Minneapolis had its own symphony and the Northrop Auditorium for guest performances of the Metropolitan Opera and dance companies, but it seemed theater-poor. The only live stages—the University Students Plays on the campus, the Old Log in Excelsior, and the Theater in the Round. The occasional Broadway musicals had to satisfy the city's needs.

The late sixties brought big changes. The tall, imposing Mr. Tyrone Guthrie (I have seen him at the University Campus Club) came to inspect our town. Several other cities competed for his Repertory Theater. I remember my delight when he chose Minneapolis. The Guthrie Theater attracted prominent actors, directors, and many local theaters sprang up.

* * *

In the spring of 1951, I received approval for my Munich medical diploma—a major worry off my mind. It felt great. Even though my coworkers warned me it would be difficult, I left the Blood Bank to start an internship. But the news about the internship didn't offer encouragement. While the German medical schools provided a lot of theory and little practice, the American students dealt with patients all along. In addition to my lack of experience and shaky English, I was a woman and a foreigner. Women doctors in the fifties were rare. Discouraged from choosing the profession, women found admittance difficult, and people expected them to either drop out or quit to get married. That wasted a spot in medical school. The few who did make it experienced distrust among patients and resentment from the nurses. Not at all like in Europe. I almost felt I should apologize for being a doctor.

Northwestern Hospital (today's Abbot Northwestern) on Chicago Avenue turned out to be a busy place with tolerant patients and knowledgeable doctors. The rotating internship took me through Internal Medicine, Surgery, Ob-gyn, Pediatrics, and the Emergency Room Service. Having other foreign interns and residents helped also.

We worked six days a week, with every other night on call. Occasionally, a resident would allow me to sleep at home, since we lived one block from the hospital. I could make the short walk in the middle of the night in safety. The salary of $175 a month was considered quite high at the time.

* * *

The night calls could be tense and stressful or blissfully quiet. On a quiet night, I could sleep, read, or go to the cafeteria in the basement. We all liked the cafeteria. We didn't have to pay for the food and had good company. We could always count on good food—the leftovers of the sumptuous dinners—available to everybody on call. A nice break for the doctors, nurses, technicians, and orderlies. I found this enjoyable but unpredictable. Any of us could carry on a pleasant conversation one minute and be at the bedside of a dying man, woman, or child the next.

I still remember being called in the middle of the night to the Internal Medicine station. A nurse had been desperately trying to get the blood pressure or the pulse of a patient. She found none. She had paged me to declare the man dead and call New York to notify his wife. After I wasn't able to get any vital signs either, with great trepidation, I began to dial the phone. I was waiting to hear the wife's voice, when the patient . . . moaned. I slammed down the phone.

The patient, a handsome, young executive from New York, had been attending a business meeting in Minneapolis when he suffered a heart attack and was admitted to the hospital. A couple of weeks after I was ready to pronounce him dead, he left the hospital fit and happy.

Another time a patient caught me by surprise. As I entered the streetcar looking for a seat, I heard a man's voice call out, "Hi, Doc. Your stitches did the job. My cheek looks great," and he kept showing it to the people around him. A few weeks before, this sturdy, young man had come to the Emergency Room with a bleeding wound in his face. I was on call. I stopped the bleeding, cleaned the wound and called his private doctor. It had been a bad winter evening with falling snow and the roads getting more slippery. The doctor asked me to take care of the patient. It was the first large face wound I had treated.

* * *

During the sixteen months of the internship (I started in April instead of July of 1951) I learned a lot. Internal Medicine had the biggest variety of illnesses and ways to treat them. Surgery I found bloody, Ob tense but happy, and the Emergency Room unpredictable. Pediatrics became my favorite.

* * *

From July 1952 until July 1953, I served as resident in Pediatrics at the Swedish Hospital. Closer to downtown but further away from our home, the Swedish Hospital had a smaller facility, less prestige, but I found it comfortable. Dr. Burgland, my mentor, was a gentle, six-foot-tall man who loved children and whom children trusted. I found him a great teacher and an excellent doctor. Later on, when I had my own children, I didn't mind travelling to the opposite part of town to see him.

Children as patients differed markedly from adults. Fearful of their surroundings, the hospital staff, and separation from their parents, they often were difficult to calm down and didn't understand medical problems or procedures. But they were honest patients. They complained when they hurt and quickly forgot about it when they got well. And I loved them. Doctors, nurses, lab technicians, anyone who had any contact with them bonded with the children. A pleasant encounter with a five- or six-year-old boy comes to mind. One morning when I approached his bed to examine him and introduced myself as Dr. Zimering, he looked at me and said, "You're not a doctor. You're a nurse."

I smiled and tried to explain, but he interrupted me and announced, "If you're a doctor, then you must be a boy."

It pained me to hurt a child, which I had to do occasionally. The children with terminal diseases broke our hearts. I remember witnessing one death. The patient was a twelve- or thirteen-year-old boy who had been in and out of the hospital quite a few times with a recurrent illness. Admitted for what seemed another short stay, he suddenly got worse. The nurse called for me. When I entered the room, he lay unconscious, thrashing around, his skinny arms and legs hitting the bed frame. Convulsions caused foam to form at his mouth and urine to flow all at once. His struggle didn't last long. Death came quickly for him, but his image remained with me for a long time.

War memories I assumed long gone, surfaced again. I could see the skeletal boys and girls, with their sad, pleading eyes, dying of hunger on the sidewalks of the Piotrkow ghetto.

42

At the beginning of 1953, Ruben liked his job, and I liked mine. We felt the time had come to plan a family. It surprised me that I wasn't pregnant yet. Some tests revealed a fertility problem. One of the tests caused pelvic inflammatory disease with severe abdominal cramps and a high temperature. Admitted to the hospital, I received a large dose of antibiotics to clear the inflammation.

I switched to a gynecologist in St. Paul who had special interest in infertility. I hated traveling to St. Paul by streetcar. Each appointment took about half a day. After several trips, many tests, and false alarms, one month my period . . . didn't come. I was pregnant! At first I didn't believe it, and then I was sure I would lose it. During the morning rounds on the pediatric station at Swedish Hospital, I made many quick trips to the rest rooms. Morning sickness with profuse vomiting (sometimes through my nose) reassured me of the pregnancy. I loved that morning sickness. The baby's due date fell in October, right in the middle of my scheduled exams for the Minnesota Medical License.

While I studied intensely with the help of English and German textbooks, Ruben ran the household. For days, the dirty dishes waited in the sink until we ran out of flower vases to drink from. The kitchen looked bad.

The exam consisted of written and oral portions. I felt I could manage the oral exam. It would involve only the patient, the examiner, and me; a calamity could remain private. The written part scared me, however. I could see myself sitting in a large room surrounded by medical students—mostly young men, of course. I would be writing the anatomy or physiology exam when suddenly . . . my water would break. The embarrassment would be colossal and danger to the baby possible. I didn't know what to do. It would be foolish to postpone the exam after studying so hard and not knowing when I could take it again. After the baby arrived, it might be a long time before I could get back to it. The only solution was to bring a towel, a large bath towel. I even carefully chose which towel I would take with me to absorb the flood of water.

Well, I didn't need any towels, the baby waited. Rosie arrived ten days late and let me finish my exams. The labor was slow and painful. When she finally arrived, I slept under a hefty dose of anesthetic. Relatives and friends knew about the baby before I did.

Rosie changed our lives. Ruben and I marveled at this human being with its tiny body, hands, feet, and toenails. But her voice sounded strong, and she saw to it that her needs came first. Her schedule became our schedule. We ate and slept when she allowed us. Her smile seemed heavenly, and her cry shattering. At nearly thirty-one, I had began to worry that I might never have a baby. I gave in to all her demands. Before Rosie fell asleep, I carried her around, sang lullabies and shook her crib. And she was a fussy eater. I didn't mind, not any of it.

To me, giving life to a human being seemed the biggest achievement possible. When I had finally become a mother, I missed my own mother even more. The three of us—baby, her, and I—would have thrived. The Holocaust catastrophe, which many had begun to forget, remained deeply embedded in me. I wanted a child, eventually more than one, to give them the names of our loved ones gone. Our children should help to fill the gap, the colossal gap in the number of the remaining Jews.

* * *

I had reached some important goals: I had survived the Holocaust, finished medical school, passed the exams and had a baby. Rosie, was the most important accomplishment to me. I faced a dilemma. I wanted to take care of her myself, but I also hoped to practice medicine. If I waited too long

I could forget most of what I had learned. Ruben didn't think I should give up medicine, but I still had my doubts.

I consulted my obstetrician, and I remember what he said: "To be a good mother, you don't have to wash every diaper yourself. It is not the quantity of your time but the quality that matters. You would miss medicine, be unhappy and possibly resentful."

I needed those words. His next advice was: "Don't wait too long with the second baby, the most fertile time is shortly after giving birth."

We took his advice. Mark arrived fifteen months later. And he was the easiest baby. He ate well, slept through the night and made few demands, maybe because by then I knew how to say no to him. Bonnie, our last child, arrived four years later.

Following the Jewish tradition we gave each child a Hebrew name after a dead relative: Rose—Shoshana after Ruben's Mother, her middle name Tauba, my Mother; Mark—Moshe after Ruben's Father, the middle name Baruch, my Father; Bonnie—Batia after Ruben's sister, the middle name Hanna, my favorite cousin.

The names: Felicia, Moshe, Rivka, Chava, Motek, Yadzia, Sophie, Henoch, Simon, Sally—of the killed aunts, uncles, and cousins still wait.

Mark, Rosie, Ruben, and Sabina with Bonnie. Minneapolis, 1959.

Shortly after Rosie's birth, I received my Minnesota medical license. My English improved, and I overcame my old fears and insecurities. I completed my internship and the first year of pediatric residency but did not return for the second year. Night calls and long office hours would have hurt our family life. I decided to work part time, working for the Minneapolis Board of Education. As a school doctor, I examined both well-to-do and poor children. I still remember a kindergartner announcing, "John is my new father. He bought me a bike." "Him?" said another little boy. "I had him last year."

Student Health Services at the University of Minnesota became my second part-time job. In the center of a beautiful campus, the doctors with various specialties cared for the staff, faculty, and fifty thousand students. Few of our patients had serious illnesses, but occasionally I found myself puzzled. One spring quarter, for example, droves of students filled our lobby. Though none of them seemed sick, they all asked for a statement of illness. After handing out a large number of the small pieces of paper, I became uncomfortable and consulted an older colleague. "I'm not aware of any epidemic. Why do all these students suddenly seem to have the same illness at the same time?"

He said, "You're right. There's no epidemic, and those students aren't sick, but all they're asking from us is to grant them some extra time for an exam. Our state university has to admit every Minnesota high school graduate, and many of them will not last long, even with our slips. But if my statement can save any of them, I'm willing to give it."

I admired my colleague's wisdom and compassion, and I felt embarrassed. From then on, I gladly handed out the small slips of paper. I hope I helped a few of them.

* * *

About ten years later, when our children were growing up, I began to think about a full-time job. I had hoped it would be at the Health Service because I loved my job and the university. I approached Dr. Cowan, the director, but was told they had no openings. I explored other options. After a long interview and some tests, I was accepted for a psychiatry residency program. Since they required recommendations, I asked the Health Service director for one. Instead of a letter of recommendation . . . he offered me a job, a full-time position in medical ophthalmology at the Student Health Service. I had offers for two full-time positions—a hard choice. I liked psychiatry and felt I would do well because of my strong interest in the human psyche with its emotional strengths and weaknesses. But ophthalmology seemed a more precise specialty, and it provided quicker, positive treatment results. And, I didn't have to leave the Student Health Service. I chose ophthalmology.

I liked the work, but I remember a few tensions. During the Vietnam War, a group of protesting students entered President Moos' office, interrupted an important meeting and refused to leave. No reasoning helped. The National Guard came, and the situation exploded. Students and members of the Guard got into physical fights. This paralyzed the campus. While we listened to the tumult, someone led in a young Guard member with an eye covered with a handkerchief. The exam showed only minor injury. When leaving, he thanked me, and I detected a southern accent. In spite of his uniform and the gun, the young man seemed quite scared to me.

After spending about ten years in the dispensary and another ten in the Eye Department of the Student Health Service, I felt it was time to move on. Since our patients didn't pay for their medical care (it was included in their tuition), they couldn't chose their doctors. Private practice, where a doctor had to win the confidence and loyalty of the patients, seemed more of a challenge. Two ophthalmologists in northeast Minneapolis had a fast-growing practice and needed another doctor. Two years after helping them on my free Wednesday afternoons, I left the Health Service and joined the partnership. This turned out to be a good match. I got along with the doctors and the office staff. The patients, many of them hard-working young family people took to me. I developed a good-sized, faithful following.

Knowledge of the Polish language helped me to communicate with many patients of the neighborhood. A grandmother once cried out, "*Jesus Christus, Pani* [Mrs.] *doktor mowie polsku* [speaks Polish]," as she blessed me and tried to squeeze a dollar bill into my hand.

43

Life for Danka and Mala also moved on. After Hitler's defeat, the Soviet Union took over Poland and imposed their Communist regime. War damage and a weak economy lingered, and the people had to grapple with shortages. I continued to correspond with them, send packages and, when it became legal, some money.

During the war, the Gestapo had arrested Mrs. Justyna for her activity in the Polish Underground Movement and sent her to a concentration camp. She survived. But, in spite of a prolonged recuperation in Sweden, her health was never the same. The two daughters looked after her for the rest of her life. Danka and Mala remained close to each other.

In the early fifties, Mrs. Justyna wrote that Danka came down with tuberculosis. Streptomycin, then a new antibiotic used to fight the disease, could not be obtained in Poland or was just too costly. I sent her the medication, food, and warm clothes. After a while, Danka wrote that her temperature was down, the cough gone, and she was slowly regaining her strength.

A few years later, Mala needed help. She had been arrested. After a court trial, she had received a long sentence in the infamous Warsaw Prison. During the war, Mala, as well as her mother and sister, served in the *Armia Krajowa*—the Home Army. Even though AK members bravely fought the Germans, the current Polish (Communist) government accused them of being anti-Communist and a threat to the regime. When they arrested Mala, she was a young wife, mother, and medical student. The family was desperate, and Danka decided to appeal. When her lawyer heard that during the war she and Mala saved two Jewish sisters, he asked for an official statement. I mailed her the required document, and Mala was set free.

Years later in the spring of 1979, I wrote to Yad-Vashem, the Holocaust Memorial Center in Jerusalem, and described what Mrs. Justyna and her two daughters did for us during the war. I asked to have Danka and Mala (Mrs. Justyna had passed away) declared Righteous Gentiles. A few weeks later, I received a reply that a special committee, after examining the case, had accepted them. I decided to bring over the two sisters.

Since they traveled alone and knew no English, our son Mark, a medical student in New York, offered to pick them up at Kennedy Airport. Mark didn't speak Polish, they no English, and, of course, they had never met. A slight mix-up at the airport scared all of them. They stayed with Mark overnight, and the next day when they saw me at the Minneapolis/St. Paul Airport, they breathed with relief. It had been thirty-four years since we had seen each other. Of course, we had changed. We weren't children or teenagers in Poland any more. We were wives, mothers, and grandmothers in far separate countries. But what remained the same was the power of our friendship.

Mrs. Justyna and a grandson. Piotrkow, 1949.

Mala, Danka, and Sabina. Minneapolis, 1979.

Rabbi Goodman honored the two Polish sisters in our synagogue. Danka, the brave one, decided to give a short speech and asked me to write phonetically the English words in Polish. After the Friday night service and the rabbi's introduction, Danka, in her modest clothes, went up to the pulpit and faced several hundred strangers. With full composure and a steady voice, she read the words of the speech. It was obvious she did not understand any of them. She expressed her gratitude for the honor, but felt that what their mother and the two girls did for us was not heroism. They only helped friends in danger. Not a word about the risks to themselves.

Spontaneous, loud applause filled the packed house. Rabbi Goodman told me later that it was the first time he had heard applause in the synagogue. (It's not considered proper.) After the service, the members swarmed around the two Polish women. Helka and I stood off to the side, not able to hold back our tears.

The official ceremony at the Israel Consulate in New York seemed more somber. Our children listened intently, when, in his moving speech, the consul said, "These two women belong to a small minority of the Poles, who, during the raging war against us and the silence of the rest of the world, risked their lives to save their Jewish friends. They are the real heroes."

When he handed them the medal and the certificate of the Righteous Gentiles among the Nations, Danka and Mala were visibly moved. We all

Mala and Rosie (in front), Ruben, Danka, Cousin Felix, his wife Marysia, and Sabina after the presentation of the Righteous Gentiles certificate in the Israeli Consulate. New York, 1979.

dabbed our eyes. Several newspapers, including the Yiddish ones, had representatives. I remember talking to a journalist from Poland. When Danka and Mala returned home the publicity continued.

Two plaques with their names and two trees occupy a space in the Valley of the Righteous Gentiles among the Nations at the Yad-Vashem, in Jerusalem. The trees are growing on a hill overlooking the ancient city. Danka's and Mala's names, together with the names of other Righteous Gentiles, are displayed in the Holocaust Museum in Washington, D.C.

I have seen the two sisters a few more times. In the early eighties, they came to visit Mala's son Slawek—a young professor of engineering at the University of Wisconsin in Madison. In the past few years, he became a good friend and occasionally our guest. The three of them came to Minneapolis, and we had a nice quiet visit, spending time with Helen and Nathan's families.

44

In the fall of 1989, after Danka and Mala's repeated invitations, Ruben and I finally visited Poland. It took me a while to decide to go back after forty-four years. I had mixed feelings. I feared opening the old wounds and facing the painful memories, but, at the same time, I was drawn to the place of my childhood and heritage.

Danka, Mala, and Mala's daughter, a chemist in Warsaw, picked us up at the airport. The busy young woman found the time to show us the city, take us to the opera, and prepare great Polish dinners. Mala's younger son, a businessman in Piotrkow, became our willing driver. We also spent time with Danka's children: her son Leszek (Lech), a professor of engineering near Krakow, and daughter Barbara, a cardiologist in Lodz. Most of their grown children and grandchildren were highly educated.

Ruben and I found the hospitality of the whole family outstanding. We rented a car with a driver and traveled with Danka and Mala to other cities, even to the famous Tatry Mountains in southern Poland.

I knew that, besides visiting our friends and my hometown, I had to go to Auschwitz, Treblinka, and Warsaw. We began with Auschwitz, the infamous concentration camp in southern Poland. In January of 1945, the Russians caught the Germans by surprise, occupied the camp and found everything intact. The atrocious sign *ARBEIT MACHT FREI* hangs over its entrance. The railroad tracks, intact, lay silent and forbidding. I could almost hear the screeching cattle cars delivering the victims. The majority of people taken here were gassed right away and their bodies burned. They retained a few men and women for slave labor. The work didn't make them free, as the big sign said. The average survival time in Auschwitz was six months.

Cattle car tracks and the entrance to Auschwitz. 1989.

Entrance to Auschwitz with the sign "Arbeit Macht Frei" ("Work Makes One Free"). 1989.

The barbed wire fence and the empty watchtowers even now, looked threatening. In one of the buildings, heaps of old suitcases with scribbled names on top, twisted eyeglasses, and worn shoes gaped at us. Children's clothes and some toys rested behind a glass wall. The old, wooden barracks of the inmates stood empty. The red brick houses, where the Gestapo, their wives, and children led a "normal" life had become offices. Instead of the

Treblinka, a large open space now. Broken rocks carry the names of vanished towns.

Treblinka. The rock with Piotrkow on it. 1989.

thick smoke with the stench of burned flesh, a breeze gently brushed my face. The well-dressed tourists walked around studying their pamphlets.

I saw it all but couldn't comprehend.

It was just as hard for me to look at the postwar Warsaw. I remembered my visit to Mother's older sister and her family in the Jewish quarter. As in smaller Piotrkow, the streets crowded between buildings; men and women in a hurry filled the shops. The city pulsated with life. I hoped that Sally, my newly discovered cousin, would soon visit me. It never happened. The war broke out, and the whole family perished.

The ghetto has long since been erased. The monuments of the young leaders, of the desperate uprising in April of 1943, tried to replace it. A high marble wall served as a reminder of all the Jews the Germans murdered. Chiseled into the hard stone, the first names, only the first names of Jewish men and women. I found names of my relatives, friends, and neighbors. I could almost see their faces. I walked away. Nearby, was the *Umschlagplatz* (a deportation place), where in 1942 the Germans assembled most of the 400,000 Warsaw Jews to be loaded into cattle cars and shipped to Treblinka.

After we left Warsaw, we headed east. As Mala's son drove on the narrow, bumpy road I almost missed the withered sign: TREBLINKA. Was that all, a simple wooden sign in a serene countryside? Was this the place where almost a million Jews had perished, where my own mother, grandfather, Aunt Felicia with her whole family, Aunt Sophie, Aunt Sara, and Uncle Henoch's wife and the three children breathed the poison gas in October 1942?

Images swarmed. I could see them being ordered out of the cattle cars onto the still-preserved huge cement platform, and, under the glaring lights, the shouting Gestapo and barking dogs chased them naked to the gas chambers. Did my once impeccable grandfather still refuse to believe the rumors?

They all arrived as live men, women, and children with names, hopes, and dreams. The poisoned gas turned them into rigid corpses, and the huge ovens burned them into piles of ashes. A cold shiver went through my body as I stood at the platform. I reached for Danka's hand and whispered: "Without your mother, you, and Mala, Helka's and my ashes would have been here too."

At Treblinka, the Germans managed to destroy the evidence of what they had done. They left a bare open space. An eerie space. Only dark, ominous-looking rocks lay scattered all over. As far as my eyes could reach, I saw hundreds of those rocks of various shapes and sizes. On each of them had been carved the name of an extinguished Jewish community, not a single person, but a whole community.

I found the stone etched with "Piotrkow" and lit a candle beside it.

Walking through the Jewish part of my hometown wasn't any easier. The narrow streets and the gray buildings looked run down, and the rows of small stores had long vanished. Not a single soul of the people I once knew remained. I went to the Polish neighborhood to see the apartment where I lived as a child and a teenager. I climbed the flight of steps and stood in front of the door. On its dark, old wood I recognized each nick and scratch and stared at the tarnished handle I had touched every day. I wanted badly to go inside, but I couldn't bring myself to ring the bell. I didn't dare. What if the people inside would rather not see me?

The entrance of our apartment building in the ghetto from which our family escaped in October 1942. Piotrkow, 1989.

The door to our pre-war apartment. Piotrkow, 1989.

218

The trip turned out to be both rewarding and painful. I surprised myself—my Polish still remained good, if a little rusty. I enjoyed the closer look at Danka's and Mala's lives and getting to know their children and grandchildren.

But the painful memories lay everywhere. I looked in vain for familiar places. Business offices had moved into my Jewish Gymnasium building, where I once studied and played volleyball. No more noisy teenagers running up and down; men with briefcases shuffled in and out. I also looked for the grumpy Jewish butcher with blood-stained apron, and the older baker who lifted the *cholents* to his ovens so easily. I thought of Mr. Gomolinski, who used to tease me in his grocery. All gone. Gone forever. Yet I lived. My guilt slipped back.

45

It felt good to be back in Minneapolis, our home. As I looked back at the years behind me, my medical practice came to mind: the Minneapolis Board of Education, the Student Health Service at the University of Minnesota, and the Northeast Eye Clinic. I loved all of them.

At the public schools, my patients were children, at the university, professors and students, and, at the private clinic, I treated whole families, many of them for years. When their grandchildren became my patients, I knew time was passing fast.

After twenty-six years at the Northeast Eye Clinic, forty-two years total in medical practice, I retired. It wasn't easy. Being needed and appreciated had been a great reward for me, and I missed it for quite some time.

Writing this memoir replaced that part of my life. I felt an instant, deep bond with my past. Writing about the war wasn't easy, outright painful at times. But after I started, I couldn't put it aside. When I finished, I felt I had fulfilled an important obligation to myself and my family.

For the few of us who managed to survive the Holocaust, life has gone on. Helen, Nathan, Paul, myself, and our spouses have spent more than fifty years in Minneapolis. We took part in each other's happy and sad events. We were amazed how quickly our children grew up and became parents themselves. The grandchildren are now the focus of our love and attention.

Above, Helen, Nathan, and Sabina. Mid-nineties. Below, Sabina and Ruben. Late nineties.

I keep in touch with the out-of-town family:

Uncle Sam lived in Milwaukee with Sara, stayed active and had many friends. He died at the age of eighty-four.

Sara, a widow now, has moved to Texas to be closer to her daughters and two granddaughters.

Felix, my cousin, and his wife, Marysia, live in New York, have three children and two grandsons.

Pola, a cousin on my mother's side, recently lost her husband and lives in Florida. Her three children and two grandchildren live on the east and west coasts.

Paul, a cousin (the brother of Pola), is a retired dentist. He and his wife, Lucy, are parents of two children and grandparents of three boys.

Helen, who lost her husband, Ben, at the age of fifty-six, remains a successful businesswoman. Her two children and three grandchildren live not too far from her.

Nathan, the youngest in the family, married last as well. He and his American-born wife, Darlene, overtook the rest of us. Their three children gave them eight grandchildren.

Two of our three children live on the East Coast: Rose and Jeffrey are parents of twins—Arielle and Tyler. Mark and Laurie's children, Yvette and Jeff, are our oldest grandchildren. Bonnie, John, and their children, Phoebe and Billy, live a few minutes away from us. It's a delight.

* * *

A few years ago Mark gave a paper at a medical meeting in Prague and decided to visit Piotrkow. He remembered Danka, Mala, and Leszek, Danka's son. When Mark was at Harvard and Leszek at MIT as an exchange student they met, became friends and stayed in touch ever since. The Justyna family gave him a moving reception. Danka and Mala's daughters, their husbands, and children traveled from Lodz and Warsaw to meet him. Mala gave a festive dinner. Apparently, her red-beet borscht with meat filled *pierogies,* far surpassed mine. Everyone pitched in and helped him visit family members in several cities. He met Leszek's wife and his two sons. One of them took him to Auschwitz.

* * *

Mala still lives in the home I knew so well. She showed Mark the wooden shed where my sister and I spent the night of extreme fear, when the ghetto liquidation began. He climbed the ladder to the dusty attic where Helka and I felt safe but couldn't stay very long. Mala took him to the empty strip of land, once Father's coal yard, as well as the apartment where we used to live before the war. Mark did ring the bell, and a friendly lady asked him in and showed him around. He inspected the once beautiful synagogue, a public library now, and the neglected Jewish cemetery.

When the journey became too hard on him, Mala said: "Let's go to Przyglow." She showed him the beautiful woods and the slow-flowing river. "Here stood the small summer cabin where your grandmother, whom you never knew, used to invite Danka and me. I have great memories of the summers the four of us: your mother and your Aunt Helka, my sister Danka and I spent together. We had no idea what was soon to come."

* * *

From left to right, front row: Tyler (Rose and Jeffrey's son), Sabina, Ruben; second row: Jeff and Yvette (Mark and Laurie's children), Billy and Phoebe (Bonnie and John's children), Bonnie, and Rose with Arielle; third row: Laurie, Mark, John and Jeff. August 2001.

223

In 2000, Mark received e-mail from Leszek. His wife was diagnosed with cancer. He asked about the latest treatment in the United States. Mark sent information and was willing to accommodate them in his home in New Jersey. He knew of leading medical centers in New York. It was too late.

Danka died a few years ago. Mala and I, both retired physicians, correspond and occasionally call. Our powerful friendship, of two Catholic and two Jewish sisters, never had a problem with the different religions. It began in our childhood, lasted through the horrors of the war and the hardships off the post-war. It wove through the lives of three generations and nurtured and protected us in the best and worst of times. Mala and I hope that our children will keep this friendship alive for years to come.

About the Author

Sabina S. Zimering, M.D., grew up in Piotrkow, Poland. She survived the Second World War in Nazi Germany passing as a Catholic Pole. In 1950 she immigrated to the United States. She and her husband live in Minneapolis, Minnesota, where she practiced medicine for the past forty-two years. They have three children and six grandchildren.